the aims of education | selected essays

THE COLLEGE OF THE UNIVERSITY OF CHICAGO

glaeser hutchinson luhrmann
pippin abbott lear warren allen

contents

DEDICATION

The annual Aims of Education Address in Rockefeller Memorial Chapel, along with this publication of selected addresses from recent years, are dedicated to the memory of Robert Maynard Hutchins (1899–1977), President and Chancellor of the University of Chicago from 1929–1951. During his Presidency Hutchins gave decisive shape to the traditions of careful discussion of original texts and the ideals of liberal learning that still animate the College. Aims of Education Addresses are published by the College in Hutchins' honor thanks to generous gifts from alumni and alumnae who celebrate his role in the shaping of our ideals.

"Devotion to truth, the courage to be independent, an enthusiastic interest in the community and in new ideas, an intellect rigorously trained and being trained, these qualities have never been in such demand as they are today. Your University offers you the example of those qualities which it has displayed from the beginning. They are the qualities of leadership. For lack of leadership the whole world is in despair. How can it ever hope to find it if honest, courageous, unselfish, inventive, intelligent men and women do not emerge from universities like this? If in this formidable territory at this formidable time you are to do your part the characteristics of the University of Chicago must become your own."

Robert Maynard Hutchins, December 20, 1931

john w. boyer

the aims of education and the chicago curriculum

INTRODUCTION

Twelve years ago, the College published a collection of past Aims of Education Addresses that met with great popularity among alumni and friends of the University of Chicago. The present volume provides a selection of more recent Aims of Education Addresses, presented over the past decade. The annual Aims Address has been a sturdy and prominent part of Orientation Week at the College since 1961. In the autumn of 1960, the then-president of Student Government, James Thomason, A.B.'61, suggested to the student board charged with helping to organize the College's Orientation Week programs that they sponsor a series of lectures on the "aims of education" as a way of introducing new matriculants to key educational issues facing them in the course of their College careers.

In its first version of the Aims project, for the 1961–62 academic year, the Orientation Board presented two clusters of lectures, beginning in the autumn quarter with talks by former Deans of the College Aaron J. Brumbaugh and Clarence Faust, as well as by Professor Joseph Schwab, on the history of the College and its curriculum, and concluding with a more ambitious series of lectures in the spring quarter of 1962 on contemporary issues facing universities and colleges in American life.

Following the experimental program of 1961–62, College officials decided that one well-conceived and well-presented lecture on the aims of education, given before the entering first-year class during Orientation Week, might be preferable to a string of divergent, if sometimes fascinating, lectures offered throughout the academic year. In late September 1962, Christian Mackauer, the William Rainey Harper Professor of History in the College and one of the architects of Chicago's famous general education course on the history of western civilization, was invited to launch the new format. Mackauer's lecture discussed the inevitable, but also productive, tensions between general education and expert knowledge, and concluded with Aristotle's injunction that "happiness lies in the fullest use of man's highest powers."

Trained as a historian of Roman history at the University of Frankfurt, Christian Mackauer had joined the faculty of the College in October 1943 at the age of forty-seven, a refugee from Hitler's Germany. His life and career at Chicago was dedicated to the pedagogical ideals that have defined our core curriculum. A year before coming to Chicago, in August 1942, Mackauer had written to a high school principal in Massachusetts articulating his views as to the value of studying history. He argued that more than anything else the study of history should not be a mobilization of ideas or facts presented in predigested formats, but rather that teachers were dealing with "the souls and minds of boys and girls. The different courses of the curriculum are as many different sets of gymnastic apparatuses for the development of intellect, judgment, character of the young people entrusted to your care." Mackauer went on to argue that "[i]t will be an immense service to the student when he learns to see clearer and clearer the deepest foundations upon which he rests his judgments, often without knowing it. The discussion of historical problems may help him to discover inconsistencies in his opinions, logical mistakes in his way of reasoning, or gaps in his factual knowledge; but it will never irreverently touch his genuine last convictions. The consciousness that sincere differences of attitude among members of one nation exist and are to be respected will be one of the most valuable results of this kind of education through History."[1]

Mackauer was above all interested in defending the freedom of the individual mind, which, in his view, could only be protected by being forced to engage in intellectual activities, much as a professional gymnast exercises to attain a kind of freedom with his body. Mackauer was a member of a scholarly generation—facing totalitarian regimes that had sought to destroy the principle of academic freedom as a fundamental hallmark of the European universities—who could no longer ignore or dodge the central issue of individual pedagogical agency for the student himself. Mackauer insisted that the heritage of European civilization had to be treated as an intellectual problem to begin with, to be puzzled over, to be understood in its deep complexity, for the good of the development of the ideal of individual freedom that was associated with the European tradition. For Mackauer, studying freedom was no longer enough. One must consciously and deliberately practice being intellectually free, and this could happen only through the active involvement of the student in the mechanisms of learning.

When he wrote this letter, Christian Mackauer knew little or nothing about the traditions of our College. But the sentiments that Mackauer expressed would have been most congenial to the men and women who organized and then defended the first program of general education in the College in the early 1930s, for Mackauer believed that students had to comprehend the complexity and even arbitrariness of received ideas in order to understand their own possible roles in modern society. Nearly twenty year after writing his letter on the study of history, Mackauer's Aims of Education Address took up many of the same themes. But his two decades of experience at Chicago prompted him also to call attention to a political-curricular fault line that was firmly established in the faculty by the later 1950s and early 1960s, namely, the extent to which the curriculum fashioned under the Hutchins College in the later 1940s had given too much weight and too hegemonic a priority to general education at the expense of allowing students to pursue more specialized studies or professional knowledge.

When the College's core curriculum was first created in 1931, it occupied the first two years of a student's program of studies at Chicago, with students then expected to declare a major area of concentration and specialization in a division during their final two years. During the 1940s, the faculty of the College gained the right to offer the A.B. degree on the basis of an all-general-education curriculum, which eliminated the departments and their specializations from the educational program of most College students. Over the course of the 1950s (and beyond), the departments then fought their way back into the curriculum, arguing, in the words of a group of department chairs from the Division of the Humanities, "[I]n view of the not too clear line between general and specialized education, some of the specialized work of the Division might [be allowed to] serve the purpose of general education and that some of the College courses should prepare the student for specialized work. Therefore the possibility should not be excluded that a student may begin divisional work while still enrolled in the College." This process was finalized in the curricular reforms of 1984 and 1998, which returned the College's curriculum back to the model on which it rested in the 1930s, namely, general education (the core) in the first two years, followed by specialization in a department or interdisciplinary program in the second two years.

The general education tradition that Christian Mackauer celebrated in September 1962 has been of fundamental importance in defining the basic culture of the University of Chicago. Without the project of general education, the University would not only be educationally poorer, it would be culturally a very different place for faculty as well as for students. We owe the men and women who first organized these core courses in the 1930s an enormous debt for their courage, their creativity, and their willingness to imagine a realm of general learning not beholden to strict disciplinary vested interests and designed to stimulate lifelong skills of self-education among our students.

At the same time, the College has become more deeply conscious over the past twenty years of the merits of the other side of Mackauer's disputation, namely, the parallel importance to our students of more specialized study and research under the sponsorship of our many excellent disciplinary and interdisciplinary majors. Today the College has fifty majors in which third- and fourth-year College students avail themselves of the intellectual resources of a major research university by undertaking more specialized studies that train them in the skills of a scholar—intellectual engagement with complex theoretical problems, dispassion in the midst of scholarly controversy, and courage in the face of intellectual uncertainty.

Our curriculum has thus come to have a strong and defensible logic, and, seen as a whole, the College is engaged in an educational and developmental process of considerable coherence. The first and the second years give our students a community of common intellectual discourse and discipline in the core curriculum as well as a rich network of friendship and collegiality in our excellent residential system. In their third and fourth years, we then ask our students to use this social and intellectual platform to engage with the full breadth of our university, with the city, and then with the world by honing their research skills and engaging in the acquisition and practice of expert knowledge.

Nor has the faculty been averse to creating new kinds of assemblages of general education courses that also advance the acquisition of specialized cultural knowledge, but in an international context. Over the past decade, the College has embarked on ambitious programs to strengthen cross-cultural educational opportunities and foreign language programs for our students, reflecting a long-standing conviction on the part of the University that knowledge of world civilizations is a key component of a true liberal education. As the great Chicago anthropologist Robert Redfield argued in 1947,

> [T]o describe this process of getting acquainted with people, with a culture different from our own is to recognize the experience as liberalizing. We are all limited in our understanding of our own[,] conduct and that of our neighbors because we see everything by the preconceptions offered by our own culture. It is a task of education to provide a viewpoint from which the educated person may free himself from the limitations of these preconceptions. We are all islanders to begin with. An acquaintance with another culture, a real and deep acquaintance, is a release of the mind and the spirit from that isolation. It is to learn a universal language.

Redfield's observation has inspired the College to create an array of civilization courses, embedded in their content and their pedagogical style in our traditions of general education, but offered by our faculty in historically and culturally significant cities around the world. In the same spirit, support for advanced language instruction overseas and student research abroad has increased dramatically. The liberating and enlightening effects of these initiatives is evident in the quality of the work our students do in their majors and more tangibly also in the fact that our College students rank in the top tier nationwide in the number of Fulbright Fellowships and Peace Corps posts they receive. Taken together, Mackauer and Redfield articulated a vision of education, conceived in the shadow of the Second World War, which continues to serve us very well.

That the College opens each new academic year with a formal statement on the aims of liberal education is thus a fitting memorial to its historic role as a major center for imaginative curricular thought and action in American higher education. The College has long been a site of thoughtful and rigorous educational experimentation. Equally important, it has profited over the generations from a sustained commitment by senior, tenured faculty in the University to teach on all levels of the College's instructional programs, and especially in the general education sequences taken by first- and second-year students. In fact, it is fair to say that at the University of Chicago much of our history—and indeed our identity—has been both shaped by and constituted by the faculty's preoccupation with the College's curriculum.

Today, the College continues to believe that the purpose of liberal education on the collegiate level is to provide our students with those empowering skills of critical thinking, writing, and argumentation, and that capacity for bold, self-confident questioning which will serve them well through the decades that follow and which will continuously enrich their lives. Throughout their four years at Chicago, our students learn to practice that civility and respect for intellectual divergence and for open-ended criticism that is one of the hallmarks of a thoughtful life, a life that strives for wisdom, for compassion, and for friendship.

Each year for the last forty-seven years a distinguished senior scholar has come before the entering class of College students with his or her thoughts about liberal education and its meaning and value to their lives. The Aims speaker is given few prescriptive instructions and even less substantive guidance, so that the resulting talks are truly a combination of Chicago-like academic laissez-faire and sheer faculty ingenuity. It is also no accident that most, if not all, of the Aims speakers have been colleagues not only esteemed as important scholars but also as brilliant teachers.

To be invited to deliver the annual Aims lecture is considered an especially high honor by the faculty of the College, and over the course of the years many different conceptual approaches and rhetorical strategies have been manifested. The challenging (and slightly daunting) invitation to reflect publicly, before a crowd of bright, ambitious, and skeptical first-year Chicago undergraduates, on the aims of liberal education, has led to a number of wonderful and memorable lectures.

We invite you to sample of few of these superb lectures in the present little book. ❍

JOHN W. BOYER is the Martin A. Ryerson Distinguished Service Professor in the Department of History. Since 1992, he has served as Dean of the College.

ENDNOTES

1. Mackauer to David R. Porter, the Headmaster of Mount Hermon School in Massachusetts, August 22, 1942.

andrew abbott

the aims of education address

2002

"Welcome to the University of Chicago." Of the dozens of persons who will say that to you during this orientation week, I am the only one who will keep on talking for another sixty minutes after saying it. I imagine that you have heard few such orations before and that will you will hear few hereafter. A full-length, formal talk on a set topic is a rather nineteenth-century kind of thing to do. Even at the University of Chicago, this is the only such oration you will get. You will be glad to know that when you graduate four years hence, the speaker is asked to speak for exactly thirteen and one-half minutes.

It's no easier for me. This is only the third or fourth such oration that I've given in my life. And you're not an easy audience. You're preoccupied with new roommates, placement tests, and "Chicago Life meetings" numbers one through five. Your minds are weary with the endless junk we've given you to read. Your bodies are aglow with adrenaline, serotonin, and the various endorphins, not to mention the more urgent excitements of estrogen and testosterone. And you are in a very diverse set of moods. Some of you are eager to hear what I have to say. Some of you can't wait till it's over. Some of you are watching the noisy dude whisper loudly two rows in front of you. Some of you are sensing the aspiration and grandeur expressed by this Gothic building. Some of you are thinking that I, the speaker, have a very big nose. In short, you're a diverse lot and I'm a beginning orator and we have an hour together to think about the aims of education. Let's do it.

It is important that you develop some personal aims of education because there is quite a strong case to be made that, given who you are and where you are, there is no particular necessity for you to study anything for the next four years. There are three basic reasons for that. They are reasons that I think a growing number of students at elite American colleges suspect, at least from what I am seeing in my own classroom. So let's be frank about them.

First, as far as worldly success is concerned, you've already got it. That your future income will be huge and your future work prestigious and honored can easily be predicted from the simple fact that you got into an elite college. About 2.8 million people graduate from high school every year; 1.8 million of them start college; forty to sixty thousand of them will go to elite colleges and universities like this one. So, basically, you and your peers at similar places represent the top two percent of an eighteen-year-old cohort. Obviously you're going to do very well indeed.

Now of course the real work predicting your future success is done not by prestige of college but by other factors—mainly the things for which you were admitted to that selective college in the first place—personal talents, past work, and parental resources both social and intellectual. The estimate of your future worldly success that we can make on the basis of knowing those things already will not be improved much by knowing what you actually do here. Moreover, admission itself sets up a self-fulfilling prophecy; since you got in here, people in the future will assume you're good, no matter what you do or how you do while you are here. And of course we know, pretty certainly, that having gotten in you will graduate. Colleges compete in part by having high retention rates, and so it is in the college's very strong interest to make sure you graduate, whether you learn anything or not.

All of this tells me that nearly everyone in this room will end up, twenty years from now, in the top quarter of the American income distribution. I have surveyed those who graduated from this school in 1975—a group considerably less privileged by ancestry than yourselves—and can tell you that their median personal income is about five times the national median, and their median household income is at about the ninety-third percentile of the nation's income distribution. That's where you are headed. And let me tell you that in the eyes of the students starting college this fall at Chicago State University five miles south of here or in the eyes of the adults going to endless night classes at DePaul University downtown, that expectation is an expectation of extravagant success. As far as the nationwide success game is concerned, there's no reason for you to study here. The game is already over. You've already won.

Now many of you, of course, don't give a damn about those other students—young people and adults struggling to move up a few notches in the middle class. You're interested in living in Winnetka rather than Downers Grove. You may want to summer in the Hamptons rather than on Fire Island. Your idea of a good vacation may be a hotel in Paris and visits to the Musée d'Orsay instead of a resort in Orlando and visits to Disney World. "Surely," you tell me, "my studies at the University of Chicago will have a big impact on those kinds of things. Surely they will determine whether I'm in the ninety-fourth or the ninety-ninth percentile of income. Getting a fine higher education may not affect my gross chances of worldly success, but surely it affects my detailed ones."

On the contrary. I have to tell you that there's no real evidence in favor of this second reason to get an education, and there's a good deal of evidence *against* it. In the first place, all serious studies show that while college-level factors like prestige and selectivity have some independent effect on people's later incomes, most variation in income happens *within* colleges—that is, between the graduates of a given college. That internal variation is produced by individual factors like talent, resources, performance, and major rather than by college-level factors like prestige and selectivity. But even those individual factors do not in fact determine much about your future income. For example, the best nationwide figures I have seen suggest that a one-full-point increment in college GPA—from 2.8 to 3.8, for example—is worth about an additional nine percent in income four years after college. Now that's not much result for a huge amount of work.

I'm sorry to bore you with this income story but I want to kill the idea that hard work in higher education produces worldly success. The one college experience variable that actually does have some connection with later worldly success is major. But in the big nationwide studies, most of that effect comes through the connection between major and occupation. For the real variable driving worldly success—as all of you know perfectly well—the one that shapes income more than anything else, is occupation. Occupation and major are fairly strongly associated within the broad categories of nationwide data. But within the narrow range of occupation and achievement that we have at the University of Chicago, there is really no strong relation between what you study and your occupation in later life.

Here is some data on a 10 percent random sample of Chicago alumni from the last twenty years. Take the mathematics concentrators: 20 percent software development and support, 14 percent college professors, 10 percent in banking and finance, 7 percent secondary or elementary teachers, and seven percent in nonacademic research; the rest are scattered. Physics concentrators are similar, but more of them are engineers and fewer are bankers. Biology produces 40 percent doctors, 16 percent professors, 11 percent nonacademic researchers, and the other third scattered. Obviously, there are a number of seeming pathways here. All the science concentrations lead to professorships and nonacademic research. And biology and chemistry often lead to medicine. But there are also many diversions from those pathways. We've got a biology concentrator who is now a writer, another who is now a musician. We've got two mathematicians who are now lawyers, and a physics concentrator who is now a psychotherapist.

Take the social sciences. Economics concentrators—this is today identified as overwhelmingly the most careerist major—are 24 percent in banking and finance, 15 percent in business consulting, 14 percent lawyers, 10 percent in business administration or sales, 7 percent in computers, and the other 30 percent scattered. Historians are often lawyers (24 percent) and secondary teachers (15 percent), but the other 60 percent are all over the map. Political scientists have 24 percent lawyers, 7 percent each professors and government administrators, and perhaps 20 percent in the various business occupations; the rest are scattered. Psychologists, surprisingly, are also about 20 percent in the various business occupations, 11 percent lawyers, and 10 percent professors; the rest are scattered. Thus in the social sciences, the news is that there are lots of ways to go to law school and to get into business. And there are the usual unusuals: the sociology major who is an actuary, the two psychologists in government administration, the political science concentrator now in computers.

As for the humanities, the English majors have scattered to the four winds: 11 percent of them to elementary and secondary teaching, 10 percent to various business occupations, 9 percent to communications, 9 percent to lawyering, 5 percent to advertising; the rest scattered. Of the philosophers, 30 percent are lawyers and 18 percent are software people. I defy anybody to make sense out of that. Again, the connections include some obvious things and some non-obvious things. We have two English majors who are now artists and one who is an architect. We have a philosophy major who is a farmer and two who are doctors.

So overall there is some slight evidence of tracks towards particular occupations from particular concentrations, but really the news is the reverse. The glass is not so much one-third full as two-thirds empty. Remember that only 40 percent of the biology majors became doctors. And, more important, remember that our alumni's experience shows very plainly that no pathway from major to occupation is ruled out.

The looseness of the connection between curriculum and career is even more obvious when seen the other way, from the point of view of the occupations. Our largest group was lawyers—12 percent of my survey respondents. Of the lawyers, 16 percent came from economics; 15 percent from political science; 12 percent from history; 7 percent each from philosophy, English, and psychology; and 5 percent from public policy. There was at least one lawyer from each of the following: anthropology, art and design, art history, biology, chemistry, East Asian languages and civilizations, fundamentals, general studies in the humanities, geography, geophysical sciences, Germanic languages and literatures, mathematics, physics, religion and humanities, Romance languages and literatures, Russian and other Slavic languages and literatures, and sociology. You get the point. There is absolutely *no* concentration from which you cannot become a lawyer.

What about doctors, 9 percent of the sample? These are much more concentrated, because of the prerequisites of medical schools. Sixty percent of the doctors came from the biology concentration and 17 percent from chemistry. However, there was at least one doctor each from anthropology, classics, English (four of them, in fact), history and philosophy of science, ideas and methods, mathematics, music, philosophy, psychology, public policy, and Romance languages and literatures. While the main pathway to medicine is obvious, it is by no means the only way in.

The other large group among alumni is in banking and finance (also about 10 percent). Of these, 40 percent came from economics, 8 percent from psychology, 7 percent from political science, 7 percent from English, 6 percent from mathematics, 5 percent from public policy, and 4 percent from history. Again there is a dominant route in, but there are many routes beside the dominant one.

I am sorry to list all these things for you, but I want to eradicate in your minds the notion that there is much of a connection between your college curriculum and your eventual career. There is, to be sure, what social scientists are fond of calling an elective affinity; there are concentrations whose graduates are slightly more likely to end up in certain careers than others. But there are no concentration/career connections that are ruled out, and there are no obligatory tracks of any kind.

So the second basic reason for working hard in some particular form of study is wrong as well, at least in this college. With the exception of those planning to become professors in the natural sciences, there is absolutely *no* career that is ruled out for *any* undergraduate major at the University of Chicago. What you do here does not determine your occupation in any way. You are free to make whatever worldly or otherworldly occupational choice you want once you leave, and you do not sacrifice any possibilities because you majored in something that seems irrelevant to that choice.

As far as performance in college is concerned, there is not, as I said, any national evidence that level of performance in college has more than a minor effect on later things like income. And in my alumni data, there is absolutely no correlation whatever between GPA at the University of Chicago and current income. Get it straight. Whether you end up on Fire Island or in the Hamptons depends largely on things that are unrelated to what you do as an undergraduate at Chicago.

I hope then to have disposed of the notion that what you do here or how well you do it has any connection with your worldly success either in general or in detail. The general level of that worldly success is already guaranteed by your admission here and by the factors that made it happen. The detailed level of your worldly success depends largely on occupational choices that are unrelated to what or how you do here.

Now the third reason for getting a college education is that it will give you foundational cognitive skills for later life. Since this is the argument I have myself made most strongly in the past, I shall take special care to demolish it.

The argument is that college teaches you not so much particular subject matters as it does general skills that can be applied throughout your future life—in graduate training, at work, and in recreation. That the actual material learned in college doesn't matter much is well known. Everyone over thirty knows that, as far as content is concerned, you forget the vast majority of what you learned in college in five years or so. But, so the argument goes, the skills endure. They may be difficult to measure and their effect hard to demonstrate. But they are the core of what you take from college.

Now what people have in mind here in the first instance are simple verbal and quantitative skills: things like advanced reading and speaking abilities that will help you deal with a knowledge economy, and quantitative training that will enable you to make reasonable financial choices and that will prove useful in area after area of professional endeavor. Beyond these lie more advanced skills: critical reading ability to see through the lies of newspapers and stock prospectuses, analytic ability to formulate complex programs of action at work, writing ability to make your ideas clear to your peers, independence of mind to free you from others' views, and capacity for lifelong learning to enable you to deal with the changing needs of work and enjoyment over the years.

There is much evidence that our own alumni, alumni of equivalent schools, and national alumni samples all believe deeply that such general skills constitute the crucial learning in their college experience. Alumni always note the *loss* of detailed knowledge from college, while they always emphasize their *retention* of general skills that they use in all walks of life.

But the evidence that college learning per se actually produced these skills is pretty flimsy. While we do know that people acquire these skills over the four years they are in college, we are not at all clear that it is the experience of college instruction that produces them. First, the kinds of young people who go on to college, and certainly to elite colleges like this one, are quite different from those who do not. If in our analyses we do not have perfect statistical control for all those differences, college may appear to have effects that in fact really originate in the differences between those who go to college and those who don't.

To this selection bias effect (as it is called), we can add the equally difficult problem of unmeasured variables. Changes that we might attribute to college instruction could actually derive from other things. College students are likely to have more challenging jobs, for example, than students who don't go to college. They spend more time hanging out with smart people. They live in an environment where cognitive skills are explicitly valued. The differences of skill could be produced by *these* things rather than by the actual educational experience of the college classroom. Moreover, since many cognitive skills *cannot* be shown to differ seriously between those who have experienced college and those who have not, much of the skill increase could come from simple maturation. You could get more skilled just because you've lived a few more years.

Our belief that college education has cognitive importance rests pretty completely on our belief that we can statistically solve these problems of selection bias and unmeasured variables, because the only nonstatistical way of handling them is controlled experiment. And no one has ever taken a thousand bright, ambitious young people like yourselves and sent them not to college but instead to some other, equally challenging, intellectual environment that did not involve classroom instruction, courses, curricula, and so on. Suppose you could spend the next four years going through a structured rotation of working internships in businesses, not-for-profits, and government agencies, where you would not be instructed in classrooms but would simply be left to pick up skills the same way everybody else there does: by asking friends and coworkers what to do, by reading a manual here and there, or by going to some organizationally sponsored classes on particular necessary techniques. You might still live in dormitories of some type. You might still have an extracurricular life. But there would be no classroom instruction. Now I submit to you that in all but a few areas—the hard sciences and perhaps engineering—you would be every bit as ready for law school or business school or management consultancy or social work training as you will be after your four years in classrooms here.

That this is likely to be true seems pretty clear from the statistical evidence that we *do* have about the net effects of college study. Let me summarize it as follows. First, there is no consistent evidence for a substantial *net* effect (say a 20 percent or more positive effect) of college instruction on oral communication skills, written communication skills, general reflective judgment, or intellectual flexibility, although there is moderate evidence for some kind of minor effect in all these areas. Second, there does seem to be consistent evidence that college instruction has a medium-sized effect (a difference of about 10 to 15 percentage points) on general verbal skills and general quantitative skills. But this seems to be a matter of "use it or lose it" rather than of learning new skills. College simply makes you keep using the skills you learned in high school, whereas many forms of employment don't. So people who go to college maintain their skills, while those who do not go to college regress. Finally, college does seem to have a substantial net effect in the area of critical thinking. However, the research on that topic has often not controlled for age, which makes it difficult to separate out the effect of college attendance from that of sheer maturation.

Now these findings are not all from elite colleges but from various samples at various levels throughout higher education. But we can still infer from them that there is not much evidence for a large net effect of college on cognitive functioning. That boils down to saying that you were smart people when you got in here and you're going to be smart people when you get out, as long as you use that intelligence for something—it doesn't really matter what—while you are here.

All of these statistically observed effects are effects of college versus not attending college, which means effects of college versus low-level, unchallenging employment or even unemployment. There is, as I noted earlier, no *explicit* comparison whatever of college with some other intellectually challenging activity. *Implicitly,* of course, we have experiments going on about this all the time. Data on the forty or so elite colleges in the United States (the so-called COFHE schools) tell us that there is wide variation between those colleges in the amount of time typically devoted to studying. There are places like Brown where it is possible to be a full-time newspaper writer for one's entire undergraduate career—treating class work as a more or less irrelevant aside—and there are places like the University of Chicago where it is not possible to do that. And, of course, within a single school some will work extremely hard on studies while others may put equally huge amounts of intellectual effort into other things like orchestra or creative writing or comedy or whatever. But nobody has yet measured those alternative intellectual endeavors in a way that could test their net effect on cognitive development as opposed to that of classroom-related work. Nor has anybody tested the probably erroneous prediction that students at colleges where large amounts of class- and homework are done actually do better later on in some worldly sense or even in measures of cognitive achievement.

So the first pieces of evidence against the argument that "college education will teach you general skills that are centrally important in your later life" are (1) it isn't really evident that these skills arrive independent of natural maturation; (2) if they do it is not clear that college education per se produces them; and (3) there is no evidence that there are not other kinds of intellectual challenges that would produce the same skills.

Now the second broad class of evidence on this "cognitive skills" argument has to do with whether these skills actually are of central importance in later life. You probably already suspect that you will learn most of what you need to know to be a lawyer, doctor, or businessperson in the professional schools for those occupations, not in college. And those of you who become doctors will find out soon enough that biochemistry and other such elaborate scientific prerequisites are of very little interest or use to practicing physicians. Indeed, it was not until well into the twentieth century that medical schools universally required heavy-science B.A.s of their matriculants. Moreover, elsewhere in the world, medicine, law, and business are quite commonly undergraduate, not graduate, degrees. So there is quite a variety of suggestive evidence implying that college-based skills are not crucial to later professional life, the opinion of alumni notwithstanding.

But let us push further. Take the standard list of undergraduate skills and run them by the occupations most of you are headed for, and let's see whether the professions really employ those skills. Recall that the skills concerned are critical thinking, analytic reasoning, lifetime learning, independence of thought, and skill at writing; these are the big five that showed up in my alumni data, that were also dominant in the equivalent COFHE data, and that feature prominently in national studies—not to mention in college viewbooks. Are these things in fact necessary in law, medicine, business, and—let's get to the real dirt—academics?

Lawyers. The real activity of elite lawyers is to find business, to make contacts, to lead legal teams, and to oversee young associates. The young *associates* need to know how to write and to have analytic skills. But too much critical thinking will get them in trouble, and independence is likewise problematic. As for nonelite lawyers, the vast majority of what they do is conveyancing, divorces, wills, companies, and the occasional personal injury case—virtually all of which they learn on the job after law school, taught in many cases by their clerical staff. That the tactics of great litigators are not learned in the classroom any one of those litigators can tell you; a background in drama is more useful than one in law. And having a deep and critical command of law itself is not useful to anybody but law professors and perhaps a few judges. So it is hard to make a case that the big five cognitive skills matter anywhere near as much for lawyers as do skills for getting along with people, for working in coordinated groups, and for clarifying and simplifying problems and selling those clear simplifications to various audiences.

In business, it is more or less the same. Those of you who go into business will never have to write well in the sense that I or some other professor uses the term. You will have to reduce things to bullets well; you too will be in the business of simplification and clarification. And you will have to work well with others and indeed will need to shelve a large part of your independence. You will have to put your critical thinking under very strict control, as Bob Jackall has so brilliantly shown. General analytic skills will be very important to you, but, again as Jackall and other students of management have shown, the crucial analytic skills for business managers lie mainly in interpreting people and in decoding the kaleidoscopically biased types of information that flow through large organizations. These are not things we teach you a damn thing about in college. Our texts are not written by people who are trying to deceive you into doing what they want.

What about medicine? The vast majority of medical work, like legal work, is in fact routine—everyday application of a standard repertoire. More than business people and lawyers, however, doctors do have to engage in lifelong learning. Senior lawyers can leave new law to the associates under them, but doctors have to keep up. Like businessmen, however, they have no need to write, unless they are academic physicians. Nor is really complex analytical thinking often necessary. The medical division of labor handles that need by concentrating those skills in a few places and referring perplexing patients to them. By contrast, critical *listening* skills—those are essential. Ability to understand what another person is trying to tell you is a foundational skill for a working physician. But we don't give any formal instruction in it at all (and indeed there is little enough formal instruction in it in medical school).

Finally, what about professors? Do they need these skills? Well, by now you've probably seen that what's really going on is that the list of "major cognitive skills" everyone talks about is in fact the stock in trade of elite academics themselves. (I should of course say "ourselves.") Critique is rewarded, analytic skills prized, writing necessary, independence and self-learning essential. To a considerable extent it is indeed true that the famous skill list is really the academics' list. Now I could make a case against the centrality of these values even in academia; most college professors work at nonelite universities with heavy teaching loads of unmotivated students and find little enough use for those skills. But even without this demonstration, it remains true that most of you will *not* in future occupational life need the specific kinds of cognitive skills that are emphasized in higher education. The most obvious example is writing.

We at the University of Chicago will obsess about good writing. But the blunt fact is that most of you will do very little writing over the rest of your lives; the major reports and legal opinions and company prospectuses and so on that you do will all be produced by committee and will be designed to tell an audience what it wants to hear or what it will find persuasive, *not* what is analytically correct.

So we have good reason to doubt not only the first part of the statement "College education will teach you general cognitive skills that are centrally important in your later life," but also the second. College instruction cannot be proved to be the source of the skills thought to be important, and, moreover, they probably aren't that important.

Let me, finally, dispose of yet another variant of the cognitive argument for college education—the notion that there is a particular body of material that constitutes cultural literacy and that it is the duty of liberal education to teach you some large fraction of that material. I call this the *lingua franca* argument, for the canon so taught is meant to be a kind of *lingua franca* between "educated" people no matter what they currently do. The *lingua franca* argument goes back to the great elite institutions of Europe—nineteenth-century Oxford and Cambridge, the Ecole Normale Supérieure in Paris, and similar institutions throughout the continent. As social elites passed through these places, they learned huge quantities of Greek and Latin prose and poetry by heart. Later in life, they quoted these phrases to each other in parliamentary speeches and casual club conversations and so on. The quotes functioned as a kind of secret code that labelled elites and also made a useful common cultural vocabulary. One didn't have to puzzle out anger abstractly. One could rather talk about Achilles sulking in his tent. Indeed, I can remember quite a few people envisioning the Vietnam War as America's equivalent of the Athenian expedition to Sicily where, in Thucydides' immortal sentences,

> κατὰ πάντα γὰρ πάντως νικηθέντες καὶ οὐδὲν ὀλίγον ἐς οὐδὲν κακοπαθήσαντες πανωλεθρίᾳ δὴ τὸ λεγόμενον καὶ πεζὸς καὶ νῆες καὶ οὐδὲν ὅτι οὐκ ἀπώλετο, καὶ ὀλίγοι ἀπὸ πολλῶν ἐπ᾽οἴκου ἀπενόστησαν. ταῦτα μὲν τὰ περὶ Σικελίαν γενόμενα. (Thucydides 7.87.6)

Yes, that's right. It doesn't mean anything if you don't know Greek. A canon works only if everybody who is supposed to have it agrees on what it is. A hundred years ago, half of you would have known what I was saying. (Maybe I would, too.) But the situation of our current educational system is that since nobody in fact agrees on what the canon is—even in the broadest terms—the system definitionally does not have a canon. In fact, there *is* a common culture of examples and rhetorical figures in America today. But most of it comes from sports, entertainment, and current events. In short, there is not an academic or high cultural canon, and to the extent that there is a canon of another kind, professors aren't especially expert in it.

Perhaps the one thing we can save from this wreck is what I shall call the gymnastics argument. This is the argument implicit in my discussion of replacing college with a rotation through large-scale internships, as well as in my noting that writing full time for a newspaper may be as intellectually challenging as doing work in classrooms. On the gymnastics argument, it doesn't really matter what you do intellectually in the next four years as long as it is intellectually challenging. Any kind of strong intellectual exercise will develop or at least maintain your intellectual skills. Since it happens that the type of exercise most easily available is college instruction itself, you might as well take advantage of it and get your exercise there. It's like going to the intellectual health club on the next block rather than bothering to drive downtown to the Chicago Intellectual Athletics Club.

The gymnastics argument was in fact at the heart of the reform of nineteenth-century Oxford and Cambridge. Nobody thought that learning Greek was going to directly help you rule India. But a person who could truly master Greek or vector calculus could be trusted to learn whatever was necessary to govern India, so they thought. Having once had the experience of extended and difficult study, such a person could master anything. At its extreme, this argument led to an absolute ignorance of the real issues at hand; many a British colonial administrator was far more comfortable with aorist middle subjunctives than with subaltern populations. But as a pure intellectual discipline it was a great idea. Unfortunately, as this example and my previous discussion of professions make clear, maybe later work is not mainly about intellectual matters at all, so maybe the intellectual gymnastics exercises are truly irrelevant.

Let me pull my argument together about what are not the aims of education before turning, in the time remaining, to the question of what those aims are. I have shown first that your general level of worldly success does not depend on your study here—indeed that success is already pretty much guaranteed. I have shown second that your detailed level of worldly success is a function of occupational choices that will come after your time here and that will be largely unrelated to it. I have shown third that there is no strong evidence that college instruction gives you cognitive skills not available elsewhere and fourth that the much-vaunted basic intellectual skills may not in fact be the most important skills either in professional school or professional life. Nor finally is there any reason to believe in a canon, since said canon is manifestly absent in actual American life. The sole thing I am willing to grant out of this whole discussion is that college instruction may be justifiable as a form of mental gymnastics. But lots of other things might serve that purpose just as well.

So the long and the short of it is that there is no instrumental reason to get an education, to study in your courses, or to pick a concentration and lose yourself in it. It won't get you anything you won't get anyway or get some other way. So forget everything you ever thought about all these instrumental reasons for getting an education.

The reason for getting an education here—or anywhere else—is that it is better to be educated than not to be. It is better in and of itself. Not because it gets you something. Not because it is a means to some other end. It is better because it is better. Note that this statement implies that the phrase "aims of education" is nonsensical; education is not a thing of which aims can be predicated. It has no aim other than itself.

There are two parts to this denial that education has aims. The first concerns the future. By saying that education does not have aims I mean that we should not want education now in order to get something later, whether that something is further education or something else entirely. The second argument concerns the present. By saying that education does not have aims I also mean that we should not want education in order to use it for something besides itself in the present.

Let me begin with the first of these. I have already shown at some length that if there are extrinsic aims of education, they do not lie in the future. Insofar as we can measure, education in the sense of college class instruction seems to have little to do with your future worldly success or even with your future cognitive functioning. But even setting aside my earlier social-scientific approach and thinking theoretically for a moment, the central problem with thinking that education has aims in the future is that the world and our knowledge of it and our ways of thinking about it will all change fundamentally by the time that future arrives. No matter what area of endeavor we consider, the facts concerning that area and the very theories and concepts by which we understand it change perpetually. Medicine, law, business, physics, architecture, farming, social work, you name it—its knowledge basis will have changed in important ways between your graduation from college and the time of your tenth reunion. Not only the facts and materials, but even the deep skills involved in these areas change with remarkable speed.

The situation becomes clearer when I state this change not in passive but in active terms. Changes in knowledge happen not just automatically, in some disembodied way, but because people *envision* them. Thus, people find new facts and materials because they look for them. They make new theories and methods because they want to replace older ones they now find unsatisfactory. But whoever we are—doctors or lawyers or farmers or accountants—we have to be able to envision these new ways of thinking about the world and of doing things in it if we are going to bring them about. So our education cannot consist of mastering disciplinary or professional material or even general skills. To the extent that you master and then reify those things—turn them into fixed, concrete rigidities—you will be unable to imagine the things that will replace them. No, to be able to transform and change and renew the ideas you work with you have to master something that enables you to see them from outside. That something is education.

This argument rejects the common idea that the aim of education is to give you the skills to survive the rapid changes in the first-level materials of knowledge. That is because the skills change, too. Writing was a far more important skill a century or even half a century ago than it is today. Now we could move up yet another step by talking about formal education at a third level—education in skills of envisioning how to change skills. But every time we move up a level in this way, we are thinking less and less about the future and more and more about a kind of constant of intellectuality—a set of mental habits that are enduring qualities of a mind. To the extent that we escape the trap that historical change presents for concepts of education, we escape it by moving to a less and less temporally directed concept of education. We move from thinking about the future to thinking about an enduring quality of the present. In short, even when we argue in this theoretical style, we do not find that education has aims in the future. Any serious concept of education seems inevitably to root itself in a state of being that endures—one based in the perpetual present of the self.

Note, incidentally, that in the process of denying aims of education in the future I have also disposed of the notion that education means learning a bunch of particular contents. I have already given a down-market rejection of that argument in its *lingua franca* guise. But the problem of the steady change of ideas (or viewed from the more active side, the problem of the perpetual need to imagine new ideas) demolishes the notion that the essence of education consists in mastering certain contents or materials. You are not little birdies sitting in the nest with your mouths open to receive half-digested worms of knowledge regurgitated by the faculty. Education is not about content. It is not even about skills. It is a habit or stance of mind. It is not something you have. It is something you are.

But now, having disposed (yet again) of the notion that education has aims in the future, I turn to my assertion that education does not have any aim in the present other than itself. I shall not argue this negatively, as I have argued so far, but rather positively, by showing that education in the sense I shall define it is a good in itself. If it is good in itself, we don't have to care much about whether it has other uses. They are mere by-products and hence of no substantive interest.

By education I am going to mean the ability to make more and more complex, more and more profound and extensive, the meanings that we attach to events and phenomena. When we are reading a text, we call this adducing of new meanings *interpretation.* When we are doing mathematics, we call this giving of meaning *intuition* and *proof.* When we are reading history, we call it *a sense of historical context.* When we are doing social science, we call it *the sociological imagination.* In all these areas, to be educated is to have the habit of finding many and diverse new meanings to attach to whatever events or phenomena we examine. We have lots of standard routines for doing this—interpretive paradigms, heuristic methods, theoretical schemes, investigative disciplines, and so on. But education is not these paradigms and methods and disciplines. Rather it is the instinctive habit of looking for new meanings, of questioning old ones, of perpetually playing with and fighting about the meanings we assign to events and texts and phenomena. We can teach you the paradigms and the methods, but we can't teach you the habit of playing with them. That's something you must find within yourself.

Now after all this buildup, that may seem like saying education is not much. “I can already do this,” you say. “Meanings,” you say, “I can give you ten meanings for your last paragraph. Not a problem. Moreover,” you say, “why should that be a good thing? Who gives a damn about all this new meaning? It’s just blowing smoke. Let’s cut to the chase.”

Well, in the first place, I’m not at all sure that most of you can play with meaning all that much. Because plenty of you are fidgeting in your seats wondering when the hell I’m going to finish. You are having trouble sitting still and thinking about one of the most important qualities of your life even for as long as fifty-five minutes. But if you’ve thought up all the new thoughts and imaginings you can generate about education in the forty minutes that have so far elapsed, maybe we had better dismiss the argument that you are—at least in this sense—fully educated already.

But the more important issue is the question of why attaching endless new meanings to things should be in itself a good thing? The answer is this: by attaching more meanings to things, by bringing more of experience under our current range of meaning and extending our range to embrace more things in more complex and abstract or sometimes ambiguous ways, we in effect enable ourselves to experience more of life in a given present, a given now. An educated person experiences more in a given period than does a noneducated person. This is not to say that there is something inherently bad or damaged about lives that lack education. An uneducated human life commands the same dignity as any other. But given the opportunity, you are a fool not to avail yourself of every means to extend your experience in the now. The quality of education is our central means for doing that.

"Bor-ing," you say. "This argument is too abstract. It's not *about* anything. What does he mean education is a way of having more experience in a given period?" Well, let's talk about something that *will* get your attention. Sex. The argument I am making is essentially the following. Any animal can take off its clothes, rub and fondle a bit, arrange its sexual organs properly, and hump away till it's done. But the experience of sex will literally be better, in the sense that it will seem to take much more time (and of course you can make it seem *interesting* much longer) if you break up the preliminaries into foreplay and relaxation, if you turn aside from the straight path a bit and graze elsewhere, if you make the thing a complex conversation of bodies referring to dozens of different imaginations in your brains, rather than just bashing away as any animal can do. That's my argument. By increasing the density of meanings in an experience, you expand that experience. You make it more extensive and more enduring all within the same social and temporal space. Education is a way of expanding experience.

If you don't like that example, consider looking at a painting in a museum. Yes, it's easy enough to look at the painting and to come up with things to think about it. But how much richer they are when you know already the many different traditions of imagining the visual world, when you can understand the detailed references the painter made to those traditions, when your immediate knowledge of the painting's social and cultural context makes you literally see dozens of things that aren't there if you don't know those contexts. It's the same argument. The experience becomes "bigger" because you are educated. Not merely in the sense that you can look at the painting longer without being bored, but also in that within a single look you will see more. And note that education doesn't lie simply in knowing the whole of the dead list of facts and contexts of who taught whom and which style was which, but rather in taking such facts as you do know and playing with them and the painting.

Now note that in arguing that "educated sex" is better sex or that educated museum-going is better museum-going, I'm not arguing that you should, as it were, miss the main point, either of the sex or of the painting. That is, because you have made the event more complex doesn't mean you have to lose the overarching sense of the simpler version. But it *is* true that you can't fill your brain endlessly—it has finite power. And so one of the crucial decisions you make about your education is how to balance breadth and depth. Because breadth too constitutes a way of expanding your experience. Complexifying is not the only way of making meaning.

Thus, I argue that education is good in itself because it expands the range of your experience, both temporally and spatially. Education means figuring out how to arrange the finite things you can know, their varying levels of abstraction and detail, their mix of skill and data, fact and theory, so as to maximize the potential array of meaning that you can experience in the now. Whatever your temporal and spatial present, education lets you live more within it, by bringing more meanings into play, by creating a dialogue of complexity and simplification, of distinction and analogy, that transforms your immediate world and reaches beyond it. To be sure, we are all bound to a reality that is local in a million ways—by language, location, race, gender, age, occupation, body type, religion, and so on. Just because you know a lot of abstract stuff doesn't mean you can escape that locality. After all being located somewhere is, paradoxically, one of the universal human attributes, and there is a provinciality of abstraction that is just as inane as that of detail. But in the mind of a thoughtful person, education is a habit that expands experience so as to overcome that provinciality by increasing ties between your locality and other human meanings. Sometimes abstraction is the mechanism for this, sometimes identification, sometimes grand simplification, sometimes the link goes through the tiniest of similar factual details, such as a similar eye color or a shared hometown.

Bear in mind too that this localism, this provinciality, is not only in space—geographical and social—but also in time. All of *you* live in a local temporality—one in which the future is your twenties and mid-life is light-years away. To you I am a fixed object who doesn't live in a now, a "professor," who was and is and always will be. But I too live a contingent life, in which things might be radically different in a very short time. To me, you are the fixed ones, who will wander probabilistically through the chances of life as I did, with just as varied results. But just as education enables overcoming impoverished localism in terms of social and cultural space, so also it means overcoming this mutual and provincial illusion of temporal fixedness so that together we can simultaneously experience the contingencies of both mid-life and youth.

As teachers, we try to entice you into this habit of education by a variety of exercises, just as a Zen monk tries to get a novice to achieve enlightenment by giving him a koan to meditate on. Note that the Zen koan is *not* enlightenment but rather is a means to enlightenment. So too there is, as I have said, nothing special about the exercises we teach—analytic reasoning, good writing, critical thinking, and so on. All the stuff of the core. They are exercises we give you hoping that they will somehow help you find the flash of enlightenment that is education. In that sense, the phrase "aims of education" is exactly backward. Education doesn't have aims. It is the aim of other things.

This "education," this flash of enlightenment, is the emergence of the habit of looking for new meanings, of seeking out new connections, of investing experience with complexity or extension that makes it richer and longer, even though it remains anchored in some local bit of both social space and social time. Everything else we teach is an exercise to achieve that.

At the same time, one should not despise these exercises. Just because I have argued that the materials and skills we try to teach in class are not themselves the thing that is education does not mean one can easily find education without them. Indeed, to invoke another, more famous, metaphor, you can think of the curriculum as the shadows cast on a wall by the light of education itself as it shines over, under, around, and through the myriad phases of our experience. It is a mistake to be sure to take these shadows for the reality, but they are something that helps us find or grasp or intuit that reality. The false notions that there *is* a fixed curriculum, that there *is* a list of things that an educated person ought to know, and that the shadow-exercises on the wall themselves *are* the content of education—these false notions all come from taking too seriously what was originally a wise recognition—the recognition that the shadows do in fact provide a starting point in our attempt to fully envision reality.

But note that in this metaphor it is not just the shadows on the wall that are not education. Knowing reality isn't education either. Education is the light, the shining thing that assigns meanings. If you have it, all the rest—the core skills and the *lingua franca* and the basic materials, all those shadows on the wall—suddenly becomes obvious. That is why so many happy alumni who found the spark of education mistake in retrospect the exercises for the reality. Once the spark is found it makes the pathway to it seem unproblematic, self-evident. For education is an invisible creativity that radiates from within. It is not something you have. It is something you are.

In summary, from a practical point of view there is no evidence that undertaking the particular intellectual exercises we set for you here at college has any exclusive connection with your worldly success or your cognitive development. Nor is there really an effective theoretical argument for aims of education going forward into the future. The reality is that education is a present quality of the self, a way of being in the moment. And that quality is its own aim, because it expands our present experience and hence is worthwhile in itself.

Three important matters in closing: First a word about the future. I have in a way deceived you with my argument that education has nothing to do with the future. I have argued that education is a quality of one's self in the present. But of course we will always live "in the present," even though from where we are now, future presents look like fixed things. "I'll be a doctor" or "I'm going to write a great novel," we say—as if these future presents were simple and fixed states of being. When you get to the future—when you become the doctor or write the novel—you'll find that your future nows are just as contingent, just as uneasy, just as "present-like," as is your present today. So it turns out that cultivating education—a sense of a self that perpetually, restlessly looks for new meanings in situations and facts and ideas—is a crucial resource for the future, because the future is a series of contingent moments just like the present.

As a result it is in an odd way true that education is your best way to "plan" for the future. (Odd because "education" in that sentence does not mean what you used to think it did.) The one thing we know of the future is that although we cannot predict it, it will happen anyway. Look at the person to your right. Now look at the person to your left. In 20 years, all three of you will have married and one of you will have divorced. You don't imagine that now. Nobody in this room, I would imagine, is planning to get divorced. But over 40 percent of you eventually will. History happens.

And these personal happenings are only one type of chance. The events of a year ago will have persuaded you that there is no escaping history. But believe it or not those events will seem quite minor in 50 years—harbingers perhaps, but not by any means the great events of the next half century. After all, nearly ten times as many people died *every single day for six years* in World War II as died in the one day of the World Trade Center attacks. The society in which most of you will die fifty or so years hence will not look at all like this society now. Widespread, everyday biological terrorism could be a fact of life, as could comprehensive economic globalization, worldwide religious war, genetic registration, disappearance of national boundaries, rationing of procreation, implanted personal locator chips—who knows what is coming?

Now you cannot *plan* for these things, overwhelming as they are. But you can be prepared to comprehend them by becoming a person who can find meaning in events, a person of education. Indeed, if you are educated you will be able not simply to experience these events, but to shape their meanings for yourself and others. You will not just experience the future, but also make it. In that sense, being educated is your best plan for an uncertain future.

Second concluding remark: I have throughout this talk considered matters of cognition. I have not talked about emotional and moral education, even though both social science studies and theories of education recognize the importance of emotional and moral growth in the college years. We do know that intellectual study will be only one of three basic activities you do here. The second is paid work. The majority of you will work on and off through college and, indeed, many of you will work nearly half time by the standards of the labor force. And the third activity is that vast body of other things—sports and clubs and love affairs and cruising blues bars and eating at restaurants and so on—that we so aptly call the extracurriculum.

Now people who think about formal education have focused on cognition and have paid remarkably little attention to what we might call the moral and emotional curricula of college, which are "taught"—for the most part—in your work life and your extracurricular life. This is not because the emotional and moral curricula lack importance. Recall that in my earlier remarks about the professions I said that professional elites often require moral and emotional skills like leadership, understanding, and organization far more than they do cognitive skills like analytic thinking and clear writing. So these are important skills indeed. But in practice our moral curriculum boils down to some brief discussions about getting along in dormitories and some politicized and often phony class discussions about race, class, gender, and so on. My friend John Mearsheimer had the guts to stand where I am standing four years ago and argue forcefully that college education is not moral education. Theoretically, Professor Mearsheimer may have been right—he argued from a strong libertarian and cognitivist viewpoint—but empirically he was dead wrong. Willy-nilly, moral learning will be central in your college experience. You will do a lot of moral learning even in the classroom, much of it learning to dissemble your real views in discussions that are more apparent than real. Sad to say, you will find this skill extremely useful in later life.

Our emotional curriculum is in an even worse state. Basically, we bring all of you here, brim full of needs and desires and hormones, let you loose on each other like so many animals in a wildlife sanctuary, and hope for the best. Why we should have arranged cognitive learning so that intergenerational transmission is highly effective but emotional learning so that every generation has to start over from the beginning is beyond me.

Now my point is that for you as individuals, your responsibility to yourselves for finding education is not limited to the cognitive matters to which the University—following Mearsheimer's argument—largely restricts itself. You need to become educated in morals and emotion as well. And in those areas, I am sad to say, we do not really provide you with anything like the systematic set of exercises in self-development that we provide on the cognitive side. So you are on your own.

Third and finally, this talk may seem to have given you an extraordinary charter of freedom. I have said—and the studies show—that what you do here has few clearly evident consequences for your future. To many of you, this may seem like a license to do whatever you damn well please for the next four years. In a sense, you do indeed have that license. Education is here to look for, but nobody can actually force you to find it. And nobody here can deny that the world is full of very successful people, at the highest places in our society, who have college degrees from eminent places and who yet lack even the most rudimentary forms of education.

To put it simply, the system as it currently exists trusts you with the whole store. Education is the most valuable, the most human, and the most humane basis around which a person can build him- or herself. And you are here offered an unparalleled set of resources for finding the flash of enlightenment that kindles education within you. But it is in practice completely your decision whether you seek that flash. You can go through here and do nothing. Or you can go through here like a tourist, listening to lectures here and there, consulting your college *Fodor's* for "important intellectual attractions" that "should not be missed during your stay." Or you can go through here mechanically, stuffing yourself with materials and skills till you're gorged with them. And whichever of these three you choose, you'll do just fine in the world after you leave. You will be happy and you will be successful.

Or on the other hand you can seek education. It will not be easy. We have only helpful exercises for you. We can't give you the thing itself. And there will be extraordinary temptations—to spend whole months wallowing in a concentration that doesn't work for you because you have some myth about your future, to blow off intellectual effort in all but one area because you are too lazy to challenge yourself, to wander off to Europe for a year of enlightenment that rapidly turns into touristic self-indulgence. There will be the temptations of timidity, too, temptations to forgo all experimentation, to miss the glorious randomness of college, to give up the prodigal possibilities that—let me tell you—you will never find again; temptations to go rigidly through the motions and then wonder why education has eluded you.

There are no aims *of* education. The aim *is* education. If—and only if—you seek it . . . education will find you.

Welcome to the University of Chicago. ❍

ANDREW ABBOTT, the Gustavus F. and Ann M. Swift Distinguished Service Professor in the Department of Sociology and the College, delivered this address on September 26, 2002.

danielle s. allen

the power of education

2001

WHAT I WOULD HAVE SAID

By early last week I had drafted my Aims of Education address. It was light-hearted, jocular. Its central subject was humor, and the good of it. But I'm unable to give that speech now.

Forgive me, then, for straying from my original plan, for you still deserve such a laughing speech. After all, you are the joys in your parents' lives and your successful entrance into a fine university, one validation of their great accomplishment. You yourselves look upon new vistas and will soon see your worlds' horizons expand at dizzying rates. Indeed, you deserve to laugh, to cheer, and to be gay at heart with the prospect of the coming years.

And so, I had intended to talk to you about the importance of laughter in the classroom. I wasn't going to put it that way, so ploddingly and prosaically and in such very unfunny terms—I wanted to dance my way lightly toward a serious point—but I was, for all the play of it, going to argue that laughter is education's catalyst. Why is it so? Because laughter is a mark or source of friendship, and friendship is crucial to encountering what is novel, alien, and unsettling, and such is the business of learning.

Let me explain. As students we invest ourselves in attending to the artifacts that the human spirit has throughout time left behind in the ongoing effort to encounter and account for the world. Our encounters with those artifacts—whether they are textual, musical, visual, or scientific—pull us beyond ourselves and the comfortable scenery of the world we take for granted. Through everything we read and study, we see how the world might be otherwise than we expect. This can be very scary. And we undertake this journey through foreign parts amid a crowd of strangers. As every course begins, we find ourselves in a room of people—teachers, fellow students—whom we do not know. We encounter one another, and our strangeness to each other, as much as we encounter alien times and places. Yet, if we are to come to understand those other times and places, to make sense of them, and to understand their relevance to our lives, we need to engage in the frankest conversation. To make progress, thinkers risk voicing half-formed ideas. They express doubts and disclose why they care passionately about particular questions. A thinker extends herself, when conjecturing an account of the world. We must, in short, speak honestly and unguardedly with strangers. This we can do only if we are confident that the others, the strangers in the room, will respond in kind—not with irony or mockery but with their own accounts and honest assessments of the ideas put forward. To have this sort of richly collaborative conversation, strangers must trust each other. At the beginning of every class, I ask my students to befriend each other, for we learn together best as friends. Laughter, shared, leads us into the necessary unguardedness.

Here let me read a strange set of instructions I happened upon this summer, which also give apt advice for the business of getting an education. They are called "Tips for Stage Coach Travelers" and were published in the *Omaha Herald* in 1877. Here they are:

> Don't keep the stage waiting. Don't smoke a strong pipe inside the coach—spit on the leeward side. If you have anything to drink in a bottle, pass it around. Procure your stimulants before starting as "ranch" (stage depot) whiskey is not "nectar."
>
> Don't swear or lop over neighbors when sleeping. Take small change to pay expenses. Never shoot on the road as the noise might frighten the horses. Don't discuss politics or religion. Don't point out where murders have been committed, especially if there are [gentle] passengers. Don't lag at the wash basin. Don't grease your hair, because travel is dusty. Don't imagine for a moment that you are going on a picnic. Expect annoyances, discomfort, and some hardship.

Here you have a set of instructions for getting along well enough with strangers to get somewhere together. The point is to generate peace enough for collaboration even in the middle of discomfort. And indeed these tips sort of apply to the classroom—especially the rule "don't lop over neighbors when sleeping"—with one crucial exception. Here in the university we *do* expect you to discuss politics and religion. On such topics, ideas are unsettling, propositions world-changing, past and present events disorienting. What's more, on a university campus, one gets the deeply unnerving sense that how one talks about the world will affect one's future actions and those of one's fellows. In the classroom, we have an early opportunity to explore how our commitments, once converted into action, will affect the people around us. This makes the collaboration involved in getting an education even bumpier and jerkier than a stagecoach ride. It requires even more effort on the point of friendship. Indeed, the effort to be friends in the classroom should become a central test of our ideas. Are they compatible with friendship? If so, then we are on the right track.

The aim of education, I was going to tell you in that original speech—the one I'm still *not* giving—is to develop an openness to the world, a way of befriending it, so that one can marshal all six of one's senses—the sixth being our mind's reason—and stretch the body taut and assimilate the world, rendering back one's own account of it in words or music or pictures or eloquent actions, an account that responds to those that others have offered, that is also true to one's own searched-out understanding of the world, and that is friendly to the world. Befriend the world, I wanted to say, everywhere. Not only in your classroom and in the imagination, but also in Hyde Park and on the South Side of Chicago. After all, this will be your world for four years. Befriend it and ask the questions about race, opportunity, and citizenship relevant to understanding it. And befriend the wide world as you travel it, asking whys, wherefores, and what nexts. Look broadly and with an open spirit.

But most of all, I was going to say, laugh. Abandon the competitiveness that so often keeps students on their guard with one another when they enter the classroom. Now that you have come to university, don't expect a picnic, but do talk to strangers; speak frankly and make them into friends. So much I would have said to you, though in a less serious tone, had we met ten days ago.

Instead we meet today ten days after so many lives were cut off. I've had to give up plotting out careful understatements and timing deft jokes. Rather than talking about jocularity, lightheartedness, and laughter, I am drawn toward a more politically pointed topic. Education has a big job to do in democracy, and I want to talk about that.

THE POWER OF EDUCATION

Last week for the first time in my life I discovered the full power of education. This sounds ridiculous coming from somebody who has herself never once in her life left school, but it's true. The aims of education therefore interest me less today than just this, the *power* of education. I present this discovery to you not modestly as a small side-effect of last week's events, nor as my own personal story of difficult times, but as a most vital discovery, equally significant for each of us individually and also for our larger democratic community. Education can ward off the paralysis of mind that is the worst danger for democratic citizens. Let me tell you what happened.

On Monday, September 10, I had given a guest lecture about ancient Athenian democracy at the University of Wisconsin in Madison and I was scheduled to speak midday on Tuesday to my host's class on Thucydides, the ancient Greek historian who wrote *The History of the Peloponnesian War*—a book many of you will read before you leave Chicago. My fellow guest lecturer, who as it happens was also my own former undergraduate advisor, was to join me in this discussion. Tuesday was a beautiful early fall day in Madison—crisp, cool, commanding blue skies. This class was going to be a special pleasure because I would again enter conversations with my old teacher and now friend.

But by 10:12 A.M. I know pretty much what has happened in New York and Washington to the people, the towers, and the Pentagon (or to the country's money and its gun). From where I stand on the street, listening to a frustratingly insufficient, tinny radio, I turn back to my original path toward the Wisconsin classics department. I go a few steps, then pause and return to the radio. A few moments more and I walk away again, only to go back to the radio. A few moments more and I repeat my departure and return. Turn and turn and turn about. I go nowhere. There is a Greek word for such behavior, this indecision, and for inaction arising from inefficiency of motion. It is *stasis*. Do you know it? Lately it has settled into my head like a swarm of bees.

The *Oxford English Dictionary* defines "stasis" as "a stagnation or stoppage of the circulation of any of the fluids of the body, esp. of the blood in some part of the blood-vessels." The word means paralysis and lack of motion. But the original Greek contains a secret that this *OED* entry does not tell. In Greek, "stasis" also carried the more common meaning of "civil war." *Stasis* meant not only paralysis but also total conflict, chaos, and confusion. How can the same word have such seemingly disjunctive definitions, meaning motionlessness on the one hand and an excess of motion on the other? Well, the Greeks knew that in a city-state when civil war was at its height, with two parties evenly matched, standing off against one another, the result is not that everything happens but that nothing happens; the very possibility of action is undone by extensive conflict.

Stasis comes to mean stagnation, inaction, and paralysis because it refers to the confusion and battling that undo the human ability to analyze, judge, and act. Plato was the philosopher who first applied this idea to the human *psyche*. In the *Republic* he argues that when our desires, our anger, and our reason are in conflict, we fall into such a state of confusion that action is impossible. He called this confusion "civil war" in the soul. Turning and returning and turning back again, my mind not working, I had fallen into *stasis*.

At least, I wasn't alone. You will remember, as I do, that in the first two days of the television, radio, and newspaper coverage of that Tuesday's events, countless people kept using the same limited vocabulary to describe their feelings: events were "unbelievable," "incredible," and "mind-numbing." One woman described herself as in a state of utter incomprehension. Everywhere people were saying that they found themselves unable to think. Minds were paralyzed, action brought to a standstill. Our inability to articulate anything beyond that was staggering. Over and over, the testimony was of *stasis*, or paralysis.

As I walked away from the radio that morning to meet my Madison host and my former teacher, I believed I could not talk to the Thucydides class. A bright still pool had settled in my head; I had nothing to say. Sensibly, though, the University had decided to stay open to keep people from panicking, and my mentor, though visibly shaken, rose to the occasion. "If we really believe," he said, "that studying these old books is of any use, then now is surely the time to test that proposition. And if there is a book with which to test the proposition, it is surely Thucydides' *History of the Peloponnesian War*. After all, it's mostly about what happens to democracies in times of crisis." Thucydides' history is a dense, tangled, and difficult account of the war between ancient and democratic Athens and its highly militarized enemy Sparta. "And yes," I thought, "it *is* about what happens to democracy in times of crisis." I sat up.

The story of the Peloponnesian War may already be familiar to you. It begins with the early history of Athens itself. The transformation to democracy got underway in roughly 590 B.C.E. when the legislator Solon decreed that Athenians could no longer be sold into slavery to pay off their debts; that assured a free citizenry. Roughly eighty years, or three generations later, in 508 and 507 B.C.E., a quick and populist revolution finally democratized the city for good. Afterward the city was run almost entirely by citizens assigned to key offices through a lottery system; most citizens would have held office sometime or other.

Then democracy grew into empire. When the vast Persian Empire to the east attacked Greece, Athens together with Sparta fended off the threat and preserved Greek independence. Athens' pre-eminent role in this conflict set it at the forefront of Greek politics, giving it the opportunity to develop into an imperialist power. The Athenians seized the moment hungrily, developing the largest navy, greatest wealth, and farthest-reaching influence in the Greek world. As the navy grew, the city became more secure, then wealthier; as wealth increased, the navy grew stronger.

Round and round that cycle went: from security to wealth to strength to security. And as the city flourished, it also grew flashier, erecting great monuments and inviting the world to visit. One of the city's leading politicians, Pericles, would eventually describe Athens as the school of Hellas (or all Greece) and argue that "we throw our city open to all the world and we never by exclusion-acts debar anyone from learning or seeing anything which an enemy might profit by observing…; for we place our dependence not so much upon prearranged devices to deceive as upon the courage which springs from our own souls when we are called to action" (Book 2, ch. 39). Athens' very openness, he argued, had produced far greater human achievements than other regimes had seen. Its success grew from its willingness to trust that the strength of collective action could overcome any vulnerability deriving from the openness of its political debate and the latitude of its laws. The allegiance inspired by this openness would be the city's greatest strength. Indeed, all around the Greek world people had generally begun to think that there was something special about democracy that made it stronger and more successful than other political systems. After all, it did seem just to keep on growing.

But the fact of Athens' remarkable growth also made the rest of Greece nervous. Finally, in an atmosphere of general jitteriness, small conflicts among the allies of both Athens and Sparta pulled the two much larger cities into war with each other. That war lasted twenty-seven years, from 431 to 404 B.C.E., attended by disease, famine, and massive casualties.

Worse, though, than all the physical disasters was what became of human relations during the war. In city after city, people took advantage of the confusions of wartime to prosecute old grudges and abuse one another; they abandoned traditional loyalties and became deceitful; they ignored the requirements and aspirations of legality; trust dissolved. In city after city factional strife arose, and in two of the worst cases, Epidamnus and Corcyra, the cities eventually imploded in civil war. Thucydides' central theme is *stasis* of the worst kind: civil war, chaos, and confusion. As his account of the war progresses, and one sees one city after another caving beneath its pressures, one begins to wonder: what will happen to Athens, to the democracy, in the midst of all this mess? What will happen to the Athenians, who depend on collective and collaborative decision-making, and open public debate, when they are faced with such crises? When the world has become so uncertain, what will happen to the people who believe that a citizenry confident in its rights is always more loyal, and so stronger, than one subject to police scrutiny? Will Athenian resilience, tremendous in peace and prosperity, find ways to reckon with the stress of war? This resilience had always derived from citizens' willingness to trust their futures to one another's hands. What would happen to that trust now?

Thucydides was a critic of democracy and it is tempting to believe that his whole narrative is leading to the argument that democracy, too, would crack, descending into *stasis* and not finding a way out. Indeed, the Peloponnesian War as a whole does end with civil war in Athens. In 404–3 an oligarchic faction, with Spartan help, takes over the city. But Thucydides does not write about this civil war in Athens. Although he saw the war end, and early in his history (2.65) mentions its end and the *stasis* of 404, his text is incomplete, stopping short a few years before war's end. Why didn't he finish the story? Is it because the democrats did in fact recover from *stasis* despite Thucydides' hints that they wouldn't? Although the city broke down in 404, a year later the democrats were able to overthrow the oligarchs and re-establish democracy, democratic legality, and the system of citizenly rights on which they had previously depended. How did the democrats manage to maintain their expertise at being democratic citizens even when stressful events led too many people to abandon their democratic commitments?

For an hour, in that Wisconsin classroom, we wandered off to Greece, to the Peloponnese, where the dry heat of the summer fills the air with the scent of all the spices growing in the landscape, where temples, exposed to the elements on every promontory, provide the nervous traveler with reference points, where the life is tied to the land and the olives, not the sea and the fish. Today I am gone wandering again, this time with you. Are you with me? Can you imagine wooden ships hugging the shore or cutting out, daringly, straight across the sea, to the craggy volcanic masses of the island city-states? Are you beginning to wonder what happened to Athens when it was at war with Sparta? In Madison we wondered and we also began asking more general questions like these: What are the strains on collaborative, collective, democratic decision-making that are likely to arise in democracies in times of crisis? Why will democratic citizens, in crisis, come to see their freedoms as luxuries rather than as basic necessities and the true source of their strength? Of what does democratic resilience consist? Are you also entertaining these questions? For an hour in Madison we wandered away from ourselves, and yet we also, with our questions about Athens and Sparta, talked for the whole hour about what had just happened to us in the United States.

I had entered that classroom bereft of thought. But in the midst of my paralysis, I began to question again. In the midst of my confusion, I began to think. Despite my grief, my mind was not numb. For an hour, by discussing Thucydides, a small group of about sixteen of us, escaped paralysis; in fact, I think, we put it behind us. We began to figure out what questions were relevant to understanding our present situation. Mind you, we did not once mention New York, Washington, hijackers, or incomprehensibility, for talking about Athens and Sparta, we found the problems of crisis in fact quite comprehensible. The distance to which the text took us was our salvation. If you now, this afternoon, have also followed me to Greece and into these questions about Athens, then the power of education is working on you. You are (I hope) being led out of yourself and into contemplation. This is something you should feel in your being as it happens, a sense of release, of slipping a trap, of anticipation; you should feel the glancing breezes of the future.

What good were ancient books on a day like Tuesday, September 11? Thucydides, in years probably worse than our own, managed to ask questions. Holding events at arm's length, he thought and wrote. He thus made art, and it does us, its readers, good in giving us room to reflect. These days we often praise immediacy, the lived experience as the richest source of knowledge and authenticity, but by turning to a text from a distant time and place, those of us in that classroom were able to step outside ourselves, outside the immediacy of pain and confusion, outside the stagnation of our own minds. Applying our minds to problems that were not our own, we gently roused our minds to life. We spent an hour talking about the very subject that was most important to all of us but without disabling our minds by attending to the immediacy of grief.

Here was the power of education: it catapulted our minds outside of this particular place and moment, and its horrors, and thank god for that, because the flight gave us back our minds. No longer did we have to use the words "mind-numbing" or "incomprehensible" to describe the effect of events on us, for we could comprehend. Friendly conversation delivered us from *stasis*. Education restored our sense of agency.

I want to turn now to the political point of this account of education. I have throughout been suggesting that what we do in the classroom is like what we do in democracy. *Citizenship is the struggle, carried out through conversation, to achieve accounts of the world that accord with norms of friendship and provide grounds for action.* We have this conversation in the classroom; we have it in the world. I have also been suggesting that democracy, more than any other type of regime, needs its citizens to have strong, resilient habits of reflection. Let me explain why.

Plato, as I'm sure you know, argued in his book the *Republic* that the best government would be one in which philosopher-kings ruled everything and there were no democratic institutions. He, too, grew up in trying times. He was sixteen when civil war first shook Athens, twenty-three when the oligarchs took over, and twenty-eight when his favorite teacher Socrates was executed. Although he wrote the *Republic* in times far more settled and secure than those of his adolescence, he nonetheless believed that democracy could not in fact solve some of the basic problems of political life. The crucial argument of the *Republic* is that politics is the business of experts. Ordinary people, he maintained, should not pretend to have the intellectual resources necessary to weigh in on matters of state. By opposing the fundamental tenets of democracy, Plato also makes them clear: democracy is based on the idea that politics *is* the business of everybody, not of experts or, at any rate, not of experts alone. Against Plato, democratic citizens must argue that an expertise in collective decision-making can indeed be spread throughout the citizenry, that ordinary people can, by talking together, reason and judge well. Democratic life therefore fundamentally depends on citizens' ability to maintain their trust and confidence in their own status and that of their fellow citizens as reflective beings. Political crises are dangerous for democracy, as Thucydides suggests, precisely because they undermine that confidence.

In times of crisis, ordinary citizens, confused and disoriented, settling into paralysis, can come to believe that, as Plato had argued, they are not up to the job of making difficult decisions. In hard times, democratic citizens may become more willing to hand over the business of politics to experts and to abandon the institutional frameworks, the rights and liberties, that secure their position as participants in the political process. The danger of intellectual paralysis in face of chaos is finally that it undermines the first premise of democracy: namely, that ordinary citizens will *always* be ready to think. To ward off the ill effects of confusion, then, democratic citizens must know in moments of crisis how to preserve their status as reflective beings. They must also know how to preserve their expertise in democratic conversation and decision-making. Finally, they must also be able to preserve their fellow citizens' commitment to democratic processes of judgment and action.

As we talked about Thucydides, we had restored to us our confidence in the status of democratic citizens, ordinary people, as reflective beings, and in the power of friendly collaborative conversation to enable intellectual progress. As we began to think again, we enacted the project of democracy, affirming that citizens, ordinary citizens, can maintain confidence in their own ability to judge even in the worst of times. *Stasis*, we realized—not plague, famine, and disaster, but chaos, confusion, and paralysis of thought—is the greatest threat to democracy. Democratic resilience consists of an ability to resist such intellectual *stasis*, just as were doing with our conversation. Above all else, therefore, a democratic education must give citizens enduring habits of reflection and practices of collective conversation hardy enough to generate subtle thought even when individuals, trying to think on their own, feel overcome. That day, speaking together, questioning collaboratively, we could comprehend.

Let me conclude by reporting what we in that classroom comprehended. Although many around us were using the word "incomprehensible" to describe what happened, we realized that once we began to ask questions again, we could sort out what was and what wasn't comprehensible in the day's events. We could, actually, quite easily comprehend the physical processes by which the towers were destroyed, and also the loss of life—it was emotionally staggering, it deserves respectful silence—but we could grasp it. We also understood that what had been attacked was not random individuals or buildings but the well-springs of principle of our political system. These things we understood without difficulty. What we comprehended less well, however, was our vulnerability. That was the first point of incomprehension: how had we, given our strength, failed to secure ourselves? Second, we could not comprehend how that failure could be remedied. These two questions we plucked delicately, once we began to think again, out of the mass the media was calling incomprehension. And when the state of incomprehension is reduced to those two questions—how did we fail and how might we remedy the failure—it is less daunting.

But our conversation about Thucydides also rescued a third most vital question. Under pressure, democratic citizens are quick to believe that their own democratic procedures—their openness, their civil liberties, their commitment to educating anybody and everybody, in short, democratic magnanimity—are part of what have made them vulnerable. The third and fundamental question is how we can secure ourselves without undoing that which, though it does to some degree make us vulnerable, is also our greatest source of strength.

Why do these principles of freedom and equality, of trusting rather than policing fellow citizens, of educating anybody and everybody, make us strong? Let me answer with a fable. Imagine you are about to go on a journey through desert and jungle and over mountains and across grassy plains; there will be typhoons and droughts and earthquakes and plagues. And as you prepare to go you are presented with a choice: you may go with one of two parties preparing to make the journey. One party is known to be free and democratic, to let individuals speak about what the group should do, to be straightforward and frank about its intentions, and to develop norms of trust and openness. The other party is known to rely on deceit to carry out its plans. With which would you prefer to travel? In the final analysis, the party that commits itself to frank openness will always have vastly more friends than the other, and vastly more consent and freely given allegiance to support it. The deceitful party will eventually find itself alone, and so too weak to accomplish its aspirations. A democracy is not weak for opening itself to the world, nor for allowing its citizens great liberties. To the contrary. It is not merely that openness and rights make us who we are as democrats; they also make us strong, for they alone inspire the consent, allegiance, and commitment on which democratic power rests. Democratic authority rests on the state's securing a way of life that we are glad to share, and on nothing else.

As, in the coming days, we consider these issues of openness and frankness and their value, we should remember the first sentence of the Declaration of Independence: "When in the Course of human events, it becomes necessary for one people to dissolve political bands, which have connected them with another, and to assume among the powers of the earth, the separate and equal station to which the Laws of Nature and of Nature's God entitle them, *a decent respect to the opinions of mankind requires that they should declare the causes which impel them to the separation.*" Those revolutionaries assigned themselves the task of proving their arguments by, in their words, letting "Facts be submitted to a candid world." Their straightforward frankness was itself radical. The author of this document understood that a commitment to open argument, frank declarations of intent, and free discussion inspires powerful allegiance, loyalty, trust, and friendship. To destroy trust and friendship, and one's status as a worthy friend, by turning to deceit, guardedness, or the restriction of freedoms, is to undo the very sources of strength that are the most remarkable democratic invention.

In the university, too, we declare reasons. Accordingly, I now welcome you to a place where habits of reflection and argument are cultivated, where frankness in accord with friendship is the guiding norm. And I ask you to see your years here as not only an educational but also a democratic experience. As you speak with your fellow students, developing each of you a strong confidence in your own ability to think, talk, and judge as well as a confidence in the ability of others to do so with you, you practice citizenship. Understand that the intellectual progress you will make here is the product of freedom and a culture of openness. Come to feel the strength that exists in the friendships you will develop in this arena of openness. Understand that their rare strength, too, grows out of frankness and fairness.

Finally, I charge you as you now undertake your own education, commit yourselves to warding off *stasis*. Commit yourselves to warding off the dangers that follow from intellectual paralysis among your fellow citizens. Develop methods of reasoning so that in moments of confusion you can, like my own teacher, lead yourself and others back into thinking. Do not let the current moment undermine your confidence in and commitment to democratic practices. No more allow confusion and disorientation to lead you to believe that democratic practices can be sacrificed without also sacrificing democracy. Restore your confidence in democratic forms of interaction—in openness and trust—by practicing them in the classroom. There restore your confidence in friendliness as a source of intelligence and strength.

Be well, my friends. My talk has been too serious, but my welcome of you to this campus is no less warm and delighted for all of that. I hope that you can educate yourselves here so that you are never, not even in the most difficult moments, found unthinking. We who are on the other side of the podium cannot "give" you such an education but only help you toward it. It's an education that you, the class of 2005, by talking amongst yourselves as friends, must yourselves win. Welcome, my friends, and be well. ❍

DANIELLE S. ALLEN delivered this address on September 20, 2001, just after the terrorist attacks on the World Trade Center in New York City and the Pentagon in Washington, D.C. At that time she was Associate Professor in the Departments of Classical Languages & Literatures and Political Science, the Committee on Social Thought, and the College. She is now UPS Foundation Professor in the School of Social Science at the Institute for Advanced Study. This address is dedicated to Josh Ober.

andreas glaeser

how about becoming a poet?

2005

You have all come here to get what is called "an education." Taken seriously, education is self-transformation. If *you* are serious, you have come here to become—to become something, or better, to become someone. If this is so, then how about becoming a poet? This is not a question; it is a serious invitation! And it is not just an invitation to the few of you who may, in the end, publish what we might agree to call poetry, but it is an invitation to all of you! For I believe there are poets in every human pursuit—in every profession, including law, medicine, and business. And I don't mean physicians or lawyers or businesswomen who write poetry on the side. I mean people who are poets as surgeons, as judges, as managers. Let me explain.

For several reasons, I found it rather hard to write this speech. Besides being intimidated by an awe-inspiring list of predecessors, I became quickly beset by a curious nausea of language. Driven by my own research about the ways in which people come to support or oppose dictatorial governments, I wanted to speak about the relationship between liberal education, pluralism, freedom, critical thinking, creativity, and democracy. This is a big subject. Many people have written and talked about it before. In fact, this particular set of terms seems to be what one nearly always talks about once the topic of liberal education is broached. So it feels—unfortunately—rather tired. Worse, the virtues of "liberal education" are frequently extolled, while a focus on skill building and achievement testing makes education continuously less liberal. "Critical thinking" is often claimed by experts, by the mass media, or by political groups while they are more or less consciously doing public relations work for agencies on whose sponsorship they are dependent. "Creativity" has become a catchword abundantly used in marketing, as well as in job-axing corporate restructuring efforts. "Freedom" and "democracy" are the stock in trade used in political speeches to justify foreign and domestic policies which end up undermining rather than furthering freedom and democracy.

As I got depressed about the depreciated meanings of the very terms around which I wanted to structure this talk, I had an idea. It dawned on me that, broadly conceived, the topic of meaning loss and meaning making provided an excellent vantage point from which I could analyze the relationship between liberal education, critical thinking, freedom, creativity, and democracy. I began to hope that this speech could somehow contribute to the renewal of these very concepts. So, here I am. Before I go any further, let me clarify two central terms of my speech. I have so far spoken about words. Yet the problem of meaning loss and meaning regeneration also affects the combination of words into jokes, stories, or theories, as well as gestures, formulas, graphs, pictures, sculptures, etc. In other words, it affects all of our symbolizations. And this, then, is the first central term of my speech. The second central term is meaning which I understand as the power of symbolizations to orient us in the world. They do so by orchestrating our interactions; conveying knowledge; exuding beauty; triggering insight; or assisting us in planning, remembering, or articulating happiness and suffering. Here is the plan for the next fifty minutes: I will begin the first part of this speech discussing the question of why the whole topic of *making* meaningful symbolizations should be of relevance to *you.* I will then go considerably deeper into this question by exploring how symbols come to have the power to mean anything at all. I will close the first part with a consideration of *how* meanings are lost and why they must be renewed. The whole second part of my speech will then turn toward what I take to be the key idea of liberal education and how, thus understood, it can further your freedom and creativity as artisans of meaningful symbolizations. Albert Einstein's special theory of relativity will serve me as an illustrative example.

ONE

It may sound strange at first, but most of you, no matter what you will eventually do for a living, will find that producing symbolizations is a central aspect of your work. The case is obvious for artists, scientists, journalists, engineers, and architects. Thinking more broadly, you will find, however, that coming up with a diagnosis in medicine or clinical psychology, that writing a report on the current situation and future development of a particular company or market, that drafting a contract, policy, or law which will actually work is just that: an act of artful symbolization. However, not only your excellence as a professional but also the quality of your life in general is vitally dependent on the quality of the symbolizations you will craft. As we all know, the good life is an examined life. For that purpose, you will have to find fitting descriptions in the world which also connect your past with your present and your future. Even our relationships with other human beings require suitable words for their upkeep and the resolution of inevitable crises.

THE POWER OF SYMBOLS

If making meaningful symbolizations is so relevant, we might really benefit from an understanding of *how* symbols come to orient us. What is the power of symbols? Interestingly, in our everyday appreciations of symbols we oscillate between two extremes. On the one hand we mock them, for example, by calling them "mere words." On the other hand we venerate them as first causes of existence, for example, in the Gospel according to John or the U.S. Constitution. How can we make sense of this?

In using symbols, we manage to "wrap" a part of the unwieldy manifold world as it appears to us into easily manipulable tokens. However, the wrapping relationship is complex. What precisely gets wrapped, even in one and the same symbolization, may vary considerably with context. For example, your answer "I will" to the question "Would somebody please close the window?" wraps only a very limited commitment on your part into your words. Yet, the very same words "I will" wrap a lot more when you are replying to the question "Will you marry me?"

Conventions and context markers help us to sort out exactly what symbols wrap in a particular instance. We know from stories, movies, and countless conversations that a marriage proposal is about committing a whole person, and we often set up or seize a context to convey that: after an extraordinarily delightful candlelit dinner with sparkling conversation, we might fall on our knees to break out into verse—or so goes one of the easily recognizable scripts. In spite of the help of these context markers, however, what precisely gets wrapped in an instance of symbol use remains principally open to negotiation and exploration. Many of our discussions and arguments aim to fix the content of wrappings. When you said to your father you would "help in the kitchen" he may have wondered "Does this *only* include doing the dishes, or does this *also* pertain to peeling the potatoes?" It is important to note that this may have been unclear to both of you. Your father's question urges a dual clarification then: to him and to yourself. His intervention alters your consciousness, however minutely.

What you will say next about the meaning of your words will, in all likelihood, have little to do with what you had in mind when you made your initial offer. What is at stake is not the past but the rest of the evening. Your reply may depend on your ethics, the strength of your ego, your history with your father, the means of conflict resolution available to you, etc. Moreover, what you might be willing to accept retrospectively as having been included in your initial offer may depend less on *what* and more on *how* your father said it. The aesthetic quality of the wrapping contributes a lot to how it will be received. In sum, then, symbols do not simply wrap what is there. Wrapping is a dynamic, even a *generative,* operation undertaken from within a life lived in a particular way, with particular projects in mind.

Much of the power of symbols resides in the fact that wrapping and wrapped exist in different forms. The word "sun" is but a small orderly trace of ink on paper or a set of brief air modulations; yet, what it wraps is in many uses a lot bigger, hotter, and shinier—it exists in an entirely different domain. To be useful, symbols *must* be more approachable, manipulable, or transportable than what they wrap. Only then can they perform their greatest feat: making present that which is absent. A map brings distant lands to us, a statue evokes a goddess which we are unlikely to behold in this life, a string of words brings back a long-gone historical event. The ability to present the absent deeply transforms the way we exist. By invoking for us now what no longer is or what only later will be, symbols make us into temporal beings with a future and a past. By calling up locations where we are currently not, they give our actions spatial depths beyond earshot and eyesight. By extending our here and now into there and then, symbols allow us to plan and to remember.

Now, remember your old Lego blocks. What makes them such a wonderful toy is that they come in different shapes and colors which can be combined in interesting ways. When you were still quite young, you were happy to mount them in any way your hands could manage. You might have named the results of your efforts something, e.g., "house for Mousey." You might have even interacted with what you had built as if it was what you called it, even though the structure had no obvious resemblance to anything you would now call "house."

As you became older, you undoubtedly endeavored to build either something you had seen or something you had mentally preconceived. For example, you might have built a Lego house resembling the house in which you lived. Doing so required not only increased skills of observation but also an increased understanding of what might be called the "logic" of Lego blocks: a growing mastery of the ways in which they can be assembled to produce particular kinds of visual effects. To become good at this, you had to take pleasure in playing with your Legos without too much concern for what it was that you might have wanted to build. You merely took pleasure in the logic of Lego blocks and its inherent possibilities.

Moreover, the logic of building with Lego blocks made you look at the house in which you lived with "different eyes" and think about it in new ways. If you were a Lego aficionado (like me), you learned to see and think Lego: you discovered aspects of your house you had not noticed before; and you asked questions about it, for example, regarding its statics, which you would never have dreamt of asking before. In fact, you always built more than you saw; and seeing with your contraption you also became aware that you always built less than actually existed. In the end, you might have become so swept up in Lego's very logic that it began to feed your imagination to build things never before beheld by any human's eyes or mind. You might have begun to make Lego fiction, enjoying it for its own sake.

Sophisticated symbol systems, that is, languages, resemble Lego blocks in significant ways. They differentiate *types* of symbols—for example, objects, relations, and qualifiers—which play different roles in the wrapping operation. And like Lego blocks, languages operate with logics of combination—which, in ordinary languages, we call grammar. Like Legos, then, they are suitable for sophisticated play. In fact, languages are the most wonderful play-sets we human beings have come up with. They easily put your old Lego blocks to shame. With different types of symbols at hand, we can build up big and complex edifices—super wrappings—like stories, formal proofs, or theories. And in language use, much as in Lego construction, something fascinating happens in the process of play. We simply forget that our symbols wrap anything at all. We begin to treat them as self-wrapping entities which derive their meaning solely from their relationships with one another. This is the step from using the figure three as a wrapping of three apples or oranges to taking it as a pure number among other numbers. We all set out on this path when we stopped calculating with our fingers; we went all the way when we became comfortable with algebra.

Through sheer play with symbols, we get self-contained universes of symbols—a world beyond immediate perception. All languages enjoy significant degrees of autonomy from the world. This affects our lives profoundly. We now have a medium in which we can pretend, work through alternative possibilities, and build counterfactuals and hypotheses; we get imagination, fiction, and fantasy. Hence, we can step out of the maelstrom of life into the medium of symbols to ponder the world. Without symbols, there would be no reflexive thought—no learning outside of an immediate context of action.

However, there are also problems with symbolic autonomy. If the world does not effectively constrain our symbolic play with its immense, if not infinite, combinatorial possibilities, then how do we make sure our play isn't just fun but also meaningful in our relationship with the world? In part, the answer is culture—complex traditions of symbol use into which we get socialized by learning a language. These cultures of symbol use often have a proven track record of producing meaningful combinations. The modes of scientific symbolization are amongst them. Nevertheless after some intensive play, we are faced with questions: "So what? Does our symbolization wrap anything at all? Do our symbols have the power to orient us?" With languages, those questions are never far away. This uncertainty is the source of our exasperation with language. It is a simple consequence of the fact that wrappings and what they wrap are different after all. Therefore wherever there are symbols, there is the possibility of doubt.

Of course the hope is always that when we put symbols to use in the world they do wrap and, therefore, organize it in such a way that we all of a sudden understand how it all hangs together. If it seems that way, we want to shout, "Eureka! I got it!" Through the use of symbols, the world—that unwieldy manifold—may suddenly look orderly, transparent, and navigable. Making meaning, that is gaining orientation through the use of our symbols, is exciting and empowering. Symbolic play brings the gift of insight and with it agency, which is the capacity for action. And this is the source of our enthusiasm for symbols as first movers. Ironically, then, the possibility of doubt, insight, and agency are three sides of the same symbolic coin.

Finally, shared symbols are literally the ground upon which we meet other human beings. They allow us to *share* in the presentation of the absent. They enable us to blend our imaginations, to communicate our thoughts, feelings, and bodily states. And thus, they make possible the coordination of our actions. Coordinated action, finally, creates the institutions which make up the fabric of our social life. Precisely because our symbols inform our actions and our actions make and break our institutions, the way we symbolize our natural environment, the family, and the state is a crucial component of what they *are*.

In sum then, symbols attain their power to orient us in the world because as wrappers they can make present what is absent, turning us into extended spatio-temporal beings; as a medium that is autonomous of the world and in which we can therefore play, they lend us the power to think and imagine; and as facilitators of social interaction, they enable us to form institutions. Symbols are integral to the ways in which we exist.

HOW SYMBOLIZATIONS LOSE THEIR MEANING

If this is so, how is it possible to lose meanings that we once possessed? Asked differently: how do symbols lose their power? For a beginning, it is useful to identify three classes of common meaning loss. The first class comprises forms of symbol *use* which destroy meaning. *Overuse* occurs when too many different phenomena are wrapped in the same terms. If everything is said to be "cool," nothing really is because the word "cool" loses its power to differentiate. Overuse destroys resolution. *Ill-use* occurs through the persistent employment of symbols in situations where it becomes rather obvious that they are misleading. If people persistently refer to other people as their "friend" while never treating them accordingly, one has reason to doubt that they mean what they say or that what they say means what we think it does. Ill-use may open an eerie gap between our symbols and our experience. My malaise in preparing this speech was prompted by the overuse and ill-use of the very terms—liberal education, pluralism, freedom, critical thinking, creativity, and democracy—I had picked as its organizing themes.

A second, very prevalent, class of meaning loss is generated by changing circumstances. Your parents' pre-9/11 map of lower Manhattan is in many ways entirely useless now. This shows that symbolizations may lose their meaning if their material, social, spatial, and temporal contexts change significantly.

A third class of meaning loss comes about because our interests, values, and ways of going about our lives change. You may soon find yourself abandoning your high school lingo with its special terms for teachers, fellow students, or subjects. If so, the reason may not only be that this lingo is specific to your high school and therefore unintelligible at this university. Instead, you may find that the ways in which you approach teachers, classes, and learning have changed so much that the old slang somehow "does not cut it anymore."

Now consider this: If our uses of symbols inform our actions and our actions change us and the world in intended and unintended ways, we unwittingly but inevitably outgrow the meanings of our symbols in due course. Meaning loss is an ordinary fact of life.

After what I have just said about the power of symbols, meaning loss is associated with losses in our spatio-temporal orientation, our ability to plan and remember, our imagination, our ability to cooperate with others, our sense of who we are, and, finally, our ability to act. Hence, meaning loss is a problem. This does not mean that all losses of meaning are bad. Quite the contrary, sometimes they are outright refreshing because they open up new possibilities for being. Luckily, symbols can be recharged with meaning. An important first step toward their regeneration is the explicit contestation of their old wrapping claims. Yet, contestation needs to be followed up with an alternative. This is so because people prefer living with depreciated meaning to living with no meaning at all. Therefore, we need to find ways to either make new symbolizations or to rewrap the old ones in such a way that they can orient us once more in the world.

Poetry was arguably the first human practice of making or remaking symbols in a self-conscious fashion, that is, in a way which is cognizant of the *process of making* itself. In fact, in ancient Greek the verb *poiein* means "to make or create." Seen in this way, poetry can be understood as the art of making meaning, the art of charging worn symbols with new meanings, or the art of inventing new symbolizations which again give us an orientation in the world. Let us call the practitioners of this art "poets." Would it not be marvelous if you could learn to be a poet?

| TWO

Orientation week is over. Now you have a pretty good idea of the possibilities and requirements of the program of study awaiting you in the next four years. Among the reasons for which you have chosen to come to the University of Chicago, our dedication to general education embodied in the common core may have had low priority or may not have figured at all. You may even have doubts about the practical relevance of such a course of study. In fact, you may feel that general education is something of a waste of time and resources because you already have a pretty good idea in which direction you want to take your education. However, it is precisely the idea of exercising yourself in a set of quite diverse fields of study which lies at the heart of what we call a liberal education. I would like to give this formulation precision and direction by claiming that *it is the key task of a liberal education to acquaint you in sufficient depth with a truly diverse set of modes of symbolic production.*

MODES OF SYMBOLIC PRODUCTION

From what I have said in the first part of this speech, you might already have a pretty good idea of what I mean by "mode of symbolic production." No matter what kind of scholars we are—whether we study Verdi's operas, whether we investigate state building processes, whether we research the genome of some living being—in the end, we do write. Ultimately, scholars at major research universities live *for* and *of* writing. We strive to produce deeply meaningful symbolizations of some aspect of the world. A simple cross-sampling of our writing will tell you quickly, however, that we write in startlingly different styles. Even more astonishing are the radically different paths we follow, the research we undertake for coming up with these writings. A mode of symbolic production is a typical path leading to a particular kind and style of writing. These modes are practiced in workshops. Some of these workshops are organized in thoroughly artisanal fashion. They comprise a single scholar drawing on occasional support from research assistants, librarians, archivists, or local informants. Others are huge operations with a factory-size machine park, a professional management and support staff, and a number of collaborating principal investigators with scores of research assistants. Seen this way, large research universities are associations of symbol workshops that practice the most diverse modes of symbolic production you are likely to find anywhere in the world. Behind the stern propriety of our neo-Gothic façades lies hidden a most colorful and noisy bazaar of symbol makers who are chiseling, weaving, carving, punching, and assembling some of the finest symbolic wares the world has to offer.

In part, our diversity hails from the different questions we ask about the world. These questions do not simply originate in an individual person's curiosity, however. Instead, they transpire from traditions of inquiry which interlace ways of posing questions with ways of answering them. In terms of this talk, they interlace the identification of meaning deficiencies with ways of meaning making. These traditions are accessible through canonized publications and organized instruction. And this is precisely where the process of producing symbolizations typically begins: with already existing writings that are either so rich that their meanings can be extended into uncharted territory or that are not quite or no longer rich enough for the purpose at hand so that their meanings need to be complemented or renewed.

And thus, we begin to formulate more questions and tentative answers. Being a scholar requires addressing these questions systematically by producing encounters with the world. For some kinds of questions, that which is sought in encounters are yet more symbolizations, say, theories or art objects; for others, they are pieces of nature, for example, elementary particles or fossils; for yet others, they are living people or the traces they have left behind in the form of garbage, ruins, or government records. These encounters are typically organized in structured ways called methods. Again, the differences are impressive. Some of us grab a laptop, a tape recorder, and whatever else seems necessary to live for a year among some group of people. Others design, organize, and conduct surveys presented to thousands of interviewees. Some of us help to build and operate huge machines to first isolate and then collide elementary particles at high speed. Yet others watch movies, painstakingly following the position and movement of the camera and the composition of the image in every scene.

What we bring back from these encounters are intermediate symbolizations often called "raw data": field notes and audiotapes; filled-in questionnaires; experimental protocols and detector plates; and tables listing movie scenes, camera movements, light effects, and color compositions. Central pieces of the wrapping work are accomplished in these encounters by describing and/or measuring carefully selected samples of that aspect of the world that is of interest to us. What follows, then, are various stages of autonomous symbolic play. Raw data are subjected to transformations which code and categorize them for easy access and further analysis. In consequence, we obtain coded transcripts, descriptive statistics, graphs, coded tables—all designating types of phenomena or variables. On these then, some further analysis may be performed to make visible connections between categories or variables. We thus get models formulated in words, equations, or diagrams. The final symbolization, the publication, minimally combines an interpretation of the model backed up with data from various stages of analysis that are presented as evidence. Thrown in are more or less detailed remarks about the research process, including a list of the literature consulted, methods and theories employed, and the data sources used.

In this highly stylized sketch of five stages as they might occur in four sample modes, I have left out many aspects which dull and spice the experience: the writing of grant proposals; the critical discussions with colleagues, students, and friends; the presentations in the classroom, as well as at conferences and invited lectures; the competition, and sometimes the feud, with rival scholars; and the extensive mullings under hot showers or during breezy walks on the beach. I have also failed to mention the emotional drama and anti-drama of it: the sublime peaks of insight and the valleys of despair; the boring grind of the day-to-day work as we plow through it.

The linearity I have insinuated only occurs in stretches of the symbol making process. Typically, each move is undertaken with the others in view. The question, for example, is more often than not posed with an imaginary answer in mind; data are collected to feed a particular analytical machinery, which, in turn, is chosen for the kinds of models it may support. The actual work also loops forward and backward between questions, encounters, categorizations, analysis, and model building. Unexpected developments, surprising raw data, or unanticipated results of analysis may necessitate iterations of the process. This forth and back shows how wrappings emerge in the interaction between autonomous symbolic play and encounters.

In sum: modes of symbolic production are techniques of wrapping the world into symbols. They are characterized by a complex movement between (1) questions posed within a tradition of inquiry, which informs what is selected as an interesting question, what can be used as a suitable method, what counts as an acceptable answer, and as a persuasive style of presentation; and (2) a process involving organized encounters with the world—particular forms of symbolic play using specific forms of categorization, analysis, and model building which pose "so-what?" questions in their own characteristic ways. They are lived in workshops which are structured by social arrangements characteristic for the mode. All modes of symbolic production aspire to be truly poetic. In that sense, good scholarship—good science—is poetry. It is a poetry you can learn at this university because—in comparison with other modes of symbolic production—the scholarly ones tend to be relatively reflective on the process itself.

FREEDOM

Why would a liberal education, the deeper acquaintance with a number of diverse modes of symbolic production, enhance our freedom? The first answer is that by moving between different modes, as well as by studying their history, we begin to understand that all symbolization is undertaken from a particular perspective. In the grand scheme of things, no symbolization is necessary—even if, for the moment, it may feel inevitable. Given other questions, other forms of encounters, and symbolic play, they might have come out differently. Symbolizations have no dignity other than their power to orient us in the world. Every one of them is better or worse for answering some questions, while remaining mute on others; they are better as a guides for doing certain kinds of things, while remaining irrelevant for others. Every mode of symbolic production is, by design, poetic in a certain domain only. That means, however, that the variety of modes we will need to symbolize the world adequately is bound to grow with the breadth of our interests and actual pursuits. Attuned to the power and limits of each mode, we arm ourselves against the temptation to reduce all modes to one. Even more importantly, however, the awareness of a choice of modes will liberate us to play not only within but also across modes whenever we get stuck with any particular way of wrapping the world. Accordingly, a liberal education may free us from the illusion that any one symbolization is *necessary,* while also making us more humble and more playful.

The second answer follows directly from the power of symbols to orient us in the world in connection with the limited meaning making capacity of individual modes. The more modes we know, the more we can open ourselves to the world. Every mode embodies a way of thinking, a way of perceiving, a way of imagining, a way of being and acting in the world. You may drive or ski differently once you know physics; you may appreciate the light streaming through the window of your room more acutely once you have studied Vermeer's paintings; you may look with more curiosity upon your own emotional outbursts once you know psychoanalysis. Thus a liberal education may awaken your desire for deeper and broader experiences.

The third answer is that the knowledge of diverse modes provides us with a repertoire of techniques of constructive criticism. The research traditions underlying each mode concentrate on a limited range of possible critical moves at the expense of others. It can, therefore, be illuminating to exploit the critical techniques cultivated in one mode to use them in others. Whole schools of scholarly work can be created by such critical crossovers. Thus were created, for example, psychoanalytical literary criticism and constructivist physics. More importantly, however, the movement between modes leads us to ask more fundamental questions about the unspoken assumptions underlying each mode. Only in contrast to other modes do they become clearly visible. Thus, a liberal education may train us in the arts of constructive critique—which is a bit like learning karate, jiujitsu, and aikido all at once.

Critique is an indispensable component of democratic citizenship because politics is strewn with claims about the world which cry out for interrogation. In response to at least the more important claims, we would want to ask: well, *how* do you know? From the quality of the questions asked and by the quality of the answers given to this question, we learn a great deal about how serious people are about their citizenship and how seriously a government takes them as citizens. Of course it is an illusion to assume that we could possibly check all political claim making ourselves. Instead, we should demand an interlocking system of independent institutions which is not only capable of critiquing the entire process leading to a particular symbolization but which *must* also be able to produce credible alternatives. Checks and balances of *power* are fine to rectify errors retrospectively; only checks and balances on symbolic production create even a chance to prevent the commitment of major errors in the first place.

In sum, freedom has four components: the relief from necessity, the curiosity about and desire for deeper and broader experiences, the ability to critique and judge alternatives, and, finally, the courage to commit on reasonable grounds. And I have not yet spoken of that last part. After we have come to know a wider range of modes of symbolic production in some depth, we should know all the better why we prefer the one over the other for a particular issue at hand. Our choice is not made for lack of alternatives or out of sheer ignorance but for good reasons. Liberal education, thus, may enable us to make reasoned commitments to a mode of symbolic production for a given purpose.

CREATIVITY

I said earlier that our symbolizations lose their meaning as a matter of course, and that we then need to either rewrap them or make new ones or both. Such rejuvenation of our symbolic work requires a lot of ingenuity and creativity. If this is the case, then how could we enable ourselves to be creative symbolizers? The precondition for creativity is the kind of freedom I have just described. The relief from necessity reminds us that we can do something; the desire for deeper or broader experiences furnishes us with a motive to act; the ability to critique and judge provide us with a road map for how to set to work; and our willingness to commit enables us to stick with it. The exposure to a variety of modes of symbolic production, finally, supplies us with a repertoire of ways to make meaning. Variety is important because, as creativity research has consistently shown, novel insight frequently occurs by transferring the wrapping techniques and forms of symbolic play from one domain to another. We call such transfers metaphors. Let us look at a concrete example of a creative leap enabled by metaphor.

This year, we are celebrating the centenary of Albert Einstein's *annus mirabilis.* Between February and September 1905, Einstein wrote a pentad of papers out of which three had a revolutionary impact on the development of physics. Most famously, in the fourth paper finished in June, the twenty-six-year-old Einstein proposed the special theory of relativity. In it, he takes three decisive turns. First, he posits that, contrary to the then still regnant Newtonian assumptions, the universe does not have an absolute spatial or temporal orientation. Instead, measurements of lengths and of time are necessarily relative to an observer within an inertial system. The second turn is closely connected. If space and time are relative to a framework of observation, they have no meaning outside of a clear measurement concept. Finally, in the third and perhaps most surprising turn, Einstein posits that light moves with the same constant speed no matter how the observer moves relative to the source of light. The postulate of a constant speed of light in conjunction with the quantum characteristics of light which Einstein had described in the March paper made sense of a number of seemingly odd experimental results on the basis of a unified theory. Other physicists, therefore, had a harder time defending the existence of an "ether," that peculiar substance that was postulated by nineteenth-century physicists as permeating the entire universe in order to account for the wave characteristics of light. Put in the lingo of the modes of symbolic production, Einstein has suggested nothing less than a rewrapping of three central and old symbols: "time," "space," and "light." He was successful because he did not merely critique the old wrappings. He offered an alternative!

In the first part of this speech, I have spoken about the generativity of symbols. By that I meant to emphasize that symbols do not simply capture what we had already known before. Instead, I said, their relation to what they wrap is typically open to further exploration and negotiation. Through a very simple example from the domestic division of labor, I tried to alert you to the fact that symbolizations produce surprises in this way. Einstein's theory of special relativity is a good example. Einstein himself used it as a stepping-stone for his general theory of relativity published a good decade later. Even more interestingly, other physicists drew conclusions about what precisely he had wrapped which Einstein was not ready to follow to the end of his life.

How could Einstein come up with the theory of relativity? First, it is important to understand that throughout his life Einstein worked from a fundamental belief about the nature of nature which he did not derive from physics. Instead, it had deep roots in his ongoing studies in the *philosophy* of nature and in his spirituality. He was convinced that nature is governed by simple, all-pervasive, economical, and aesthetically appealing principles. For Einstein, nature was materialized reason, an imminent God. In all likelihood, he gleaned this understanding of matter from his readings of enlightenment philosophy, Spinoza above all. These readings date back well into his high school years, and they were continued throughout his studies in Zürich and among a circle of friends during his years as a patent officer in Bern. On the basis of his beliefs about nature, he felt that asymmetries in the explanation of natural phenomena were intolerable. One such asymmetry marred for Einstein the theory of electrodynamics, which was widely considered the crowning achievement of nineteenth-century physics. Maxwell, its finishing architect, offered two discrepant accounts of how a magnet rotating in a coil—or a coil rotating around a magnet—produces an electric current. Such asymmetries, along with seemingly inexplicable experimental results, offended Einstein's spiritual-aesthetic sensibilities, thus motivating his work. Philosophy also influenced the way he found his solutions; he was convinced that such problems could only be resolved on the basis of principles of a higher generality. And this is what he set out to do—*more geometrico.*

As far as the relativity of time and space is concerned, Einstein was greatly influenced by more than the philosophical writings of Hume, Mach, and Poincaré. Clock synchronization, the centerpiece of Einstein's concept of time, was a prevalent engineering concern in the late nineteenth and early twentieth centuries. Einstein himself had evaluated several patents offering solutions to this problem. His emphasis on measurement procedure was also inspired as much by philosophy as by his nitty-gritty work as a patent officer with its emphasis on the demonstrability of claimed effects. Finally, it bears mentioning that during his high school years in Munich, Einstein was an avid reader of popular science books which made much use of imaginary rides, for example, on light waves. This form of imagination was constantly employed by Einstein as a thinking tool.

Einstein's theory emerged, then, in the interstices between various modes of symbolic production. His fundamental motivating assumptions are metaphysical in style. His mode of reasoning is hypothetical-deductive, in the manner of philosophy or mathematics, which is, in addition, shot through with entirely (science-) fictional examples that are often somewhat shamefacedly called "thought experiments." Yet he employs this reasoning to make sense of inductively, that is, experimentally generated puzzles which have offended his spiritual-aesthetic assumptions. Finally, he mingles engineering sensibilities about measurement and demonstrability with those of positivist philosophy to inform his formulations of concepts. Einstein's genius is one of carrying over modes of symbolic production from one domain to another, and connecting them to a problem which he studied with great perseverance. His ingenuity is based on finding and focusing several metaphors on one problem.

Einstein worked and thought for years about a related set of problems. And he did so in close collaboration with others—with a few good friends, and, especially, with his wife. According to his own account, the very breakthrough emerged after a full day of discussions with an old friend. Two aspects of this story strike me as important. Symbolization needs to be done and redone with others who affirm us, challenge us, and offer us a space in which we can play with our symbolizations with almost no risks to our material well-being or social status. Yet, the creative leap occurs in seclusion from others, in the silent dialogue of a self within itself. Then, Einstein was a liminal person—someone who was socially located at the boundary between different worlds. Outside of a traditional university context, he could take his work where he, not his professors, wanted to go. He lived in Switzerland as a German; a Swabian, he grew up among Bavarians; among Swabians, he was a Jew; and among Jews, he was secular. Einstein was an expert in living in the spaces between worlds; in fact, he clearly came to relish it as a liberating opportunity.

Let me draw a final lesson from this example. Diverse modes of symbolic production are not just characteristic of various academic fields, but they are constitutive of religions and cultures. Luckily, a top international research university such as this one attracts students from all over the world, not only from most walks of society in the United States. As a bazaar of symbol workshops, such a university is surrounded by residential quarters that are rich in diverse symbol-making traditions. They are yours to explore with as much interest and intensity as the academic modes of symbolic production. Learning about them is just as revealing. Clearly you could get by in these quarters using the generally accepted *lingua franca* of the place: English. But you would get only so far in understanding other cultures without learning their prime vehicle of symbolization: their language. Learning a language which does not share the fundamental structural characteristics of your own is an especially eye-opening experience for anybody interested in how differently we can wrap the world. For that reason alone, a liberal education in the sense discussed here is quite incomplete without acquiring fluency in at least one foreign language.

I have not found any investigation which directly demonstrates that liberal education *does* make people more creative. And yet, there is significant evidence that Einstein's story, his metaphoric focusing enabled by his liminal position, is rather typical for creative insight. Beyond the biographic study of creative individuals, there is strong evidence from investigations lodged at a higher level of social organization. First, there is positive evidence. Creativity often comes in bursts across many fields at the same time, concentrated in dense, cosmopolitan cities. Classical Athens in the late fifth and early fourth centuries, and Pataliputra (today's Patna) in the third century B.C.E. were such places; so were Fes in the fourteenth and Florence in the fifteenth centuries. Vienna and Tokyo saw such a burst at the turn from the nineteenth to the twentieth century. Today, New York is, perhaps more than any other city—sorry, Chicago!—such an incubator of creativity. However, cities, even very diverse ones, are not necessarily creative hubs at all times. For cities to become fermenters of creativity, they need to become places of engagement between people with different ideas working with different modes of symbolic production. For that they need to offer people with diverse backgrounds several things. They need real career opportunities which allow them to become symbolically productive. And then they need an infrastructure of meeting places ranging from cafés to political, artistic, and scientific institutions, which facilitate a free, open-minded exchange between various modes of symbolic production thus sparking metaphors.

Second, there is negative evidence. And this is where my own research into the reasons why and how socialism collapsed becomes important. In the political and economic realm, socialism took great pains to homogenize its population. The idea was that the science of dialectical materialism had discovered the true laws of history and of human society. If only everybody could be taught Marxism-Leninism and be persuaded to act accordingly, then socialism would come true as a self-fulfilling prophecy. Humankind would thus catapult itself into communism, the only conceivable just human order. At the same time, socialism thought itself embroiled in mortal combat with capitalism. All forces had to be mobilized in unity to fight the enemy. Although the praise of critique was universally sung, this had the effect of causing the actual practice of critique to be generally read as a diversion from the main task—the defeat of the enemy. Accordingly, critique was seen as a mere nuisance, a carping about, which was effectively in the interest of the enemy. Unity and unwavering support for party and state became the ethical ideal. In the interest of efficiency at war, pluralism was seen at best as an unnecessary luxury and at worst as an ideological floodgate for the forces of evil. In this call to unity in battle, armed with the supposed truth, socialism literally suffocated. It had no way left to determine whether or not its own symbolizations of itself still had any bearing on lived life, whether its symbolizations were still offering useful orientation. During the 1980s in particular, the self-praise of party and government began to deviate from experience. The economic plans were always advertised as over-fulfilled while people experienced increased shortages. An eerie gap opened between what was said about the country and what people experienced—a gap that was increasingly appreciated even by the party elites who saw the erosion of meaning with increasing alarm. Yet, they had no way to develop alternative symbolizations which would immediately have been read as subversive. Ossified institutionally, they had no way to regenerate meaning. Once the crisis accelerated in 1989, the governing elites literally had nothing to say and, therefore, no clue what to do. And thus, symbolically exhausted, they forfeited power without firing a single shot!

The biographies of innovative people, the creativity generating possibilities of cosmopolitan centers, and the political self-suffocation of socialism offer important lessons for *all* social arrangements. A pluralism of modes of symbolization, practiced in a multitude of symbol workshops enabled and freed to engage in creative borrowing from each other, is the very precondition for the regeneration of meaning under conditions of rapid social change in which meanings are lost just as fast. In an important sense, every mode of symbolization can be looked at as a culture. If this is so, then multiculturalism is not only not dead—or dangerous, as more and more politicians and intellectuals in Europe and America have recently claimed—but it is necessary for the continuous rejuvenation of meaning. Multiculturalism is an asset, not a liability. Perhaps I should say that it must be *made* into an asset, for multiculturalism needs to be *practiced* and not just preached to yield the fruits of freedom and creativity. We urgently need people who, like Einstein, can thrive in a multicultural environment, who relish rather than abhor it, who see it as a liberating opportunity rather than an anxiety-provoking nightmare. We need people who are free in the sense I have defined it just a few minutes ago. Liberal education is one of our best bets at nourishing such sensibilities by creating plenty of opportunities for becoming comfortable with leading a liminal life.

Throughout my speech, I have said that liberal education *may* make people more free and creative. For it does not do so automatically. You can live in the middle of a cosmopolitan city and remain entirely untouched by the diversity of modes of symbolization practiced there. You can go through a curriculum of liberal education without reaping any of its potential benefits. You can learn many modes of thought without ever making any metaphoric linkages between them. For this to happen, you need only to think that all those things around you are either neatly compartmentalized or in an important sense external to you and should remain so. Tourists, diplomats, and representatives of corporations often do that when they go to other countries—merely enjoying the titillation of the exotic while never letting anything come really close. The philosopher John Dewey once called such people "cosmopolitan idiots." They look educated, but they are mere kaleidoscopes of knowledges which they employ for their parochial agendas.

The point is not only to avoid becoming a cosmopolitan idiot but also to become a free symbol maker who is ready and eager to participate in the creative rejuvenation of meaning. For this to happen, you can not just surf on diverse modes of symbolic production—scientific, artistic, religious, or cultural. Instead, you *must* delve into them and engage with them to such a degree and at such a proximity, that they, in fact, stand a chance to alter the way in which you think, feel, act, dream, and imagine.

To reap the benefits of diversity, you must *risk* yourself—ready to become transformed in the course of the engagement. This does not mean that you have to make your own all of the modes of symbolic production which you encounter on the way. You will undoubtedly find some of them misguided or even wrong. But you should know why. The point is that by fathoming the operations of diverse modes and by wrestling with their limits and possibilities, you stand a very good chance of becoming a freer and more creative person.

You stand at the gates of a splendid university—a wondrous metropolis of symbol makers ready for you to explore. Fearlessly walking its many streets, watching and listening intently, and asking questions with curious abandon may eventually make you want to participate. It may kindle in you a passion for making deeply meaningful symbolizations, those which orient us in the world by enhancing our power to think, our power to experience deeply and reflexively, our power to imagine, and, thus, ultimately our power to live better lives. You *could* become a poet. And where, if not here; and when, if not now? Welcome to the University of Chicago. ❍

ANDREAS GLAESER, Associate Professor in the Department of Sociology and the College, delivered this address on September 22, 2005.

dennis j. hutchinson

the aims of education address

1999

There is no greater privilege for a teacher here than to deliver the Aims of Education Address: no topic is more important, no other academic event gathers every member of the class under one roof, and no other setting on campus better weds the ambitions of architecture with occasion. I cannot explore all of the aims of every part of your education, of course, but perhaps like the choirmaster's pitch pipe before the concert, I can momentarily strike a helpful note.

Eight years ago, a first-year student whom I will call Rachael sat in these pews and listened to one of my colleagues exemplify the Aims of Education by explicating a poem. She went on to graduate with a degree in English and then crossed the Midway where she graduated last June from the Law School. Several weeks ago, she was summoned for a job interview by the Chief Justice of the United States, who was considering whether to hire her as one of his three clerks. The Chief Justice reviewed her résumé and remarked in passing that the College curriculum had been "in the news." "What did you get out of it?" he asked her.

"It taught me to think," she replied evenly.

"Well," responded the Chief Justice, "most people say that about law school."

Pausing for a polite breath, she said: "Chicago is different."

"So it is," the Chief Justice agreed, in what apparently was intended as both an acknowledgment and a compliment to the College—and not necessarily at the expense of the Law School.

Later, I asked Rachael to explain to me what she meant or, more precisely, what a more complete answer to the Chief Justice would have been. This is what she wrote to me:

> I think the act of learning how to think rather than the ultimate learning on the actual subject matter was what I really took away from the whole experience. I couldn't discuss the categorical imperative effectively at this point. I probably couldn't offer more than a sentence or two on the Wealth of Nations or the Communist Manifesto. I certainly can't tell you whether the Mesozoic period came before or after Cretaceous. But I did learn intellectual discipline and an enthusiasm for tackling future scholarly enterprises. . . . [I]t turned out to be law (for now at least) but I feel comfortable that it could have been almost anything else and I would have been well-equipped.[1]

Rachael's testimony and the Chief Justice's remark are the latest variations on a theme which now stretches back for decades and which suggests more than coincidence. Some years ago, graduates of the College who were pursuing advanced work at Stanford were said by administrators to be impressive for

> their unique and recognizable intellectual style. This showed itself most typically as a habit of phrasing and then revising questions and attempted answers, a habit that sometimes

> extended to offering, helpfully if not always endearingly, to rephrase the questions and statements of their elders.[2]

More recently, the president of another university told me that "Chicago graduates have a cutting edge and clarity that is distinct, full value, and sometimes uncomfortably direct."

There is more evidence in the same vein, although it, too, is anecdotal and perhaps subject to some discount. Nonetheless, assume for the moment that the quoted witnesses are on to something. What could account for a "unique and recognizable intellectual style" which meets the most demanding standards of rigor? The Dean of the College has rightly dismissed one possible explanation—"the raw numbers of required elementary courses we demand of our students."[3] Hard work and lots of it does not necessarily produce a cast of mind, because the work could consist simply of memorization or the acquisition of data or the absorption of the views of others.

Obviously, the content of the curriculum is more important than its gross tonnage. So is the "Chicago style" the product of an ingenious curricular design? Some would like to believe that, but as my late colleague Phil Kurland liked to say, in his own direct style, "simple solutions appeal only to the simple-minded." Our curriculum is actually a succession of rather different structures spanning the last seventy years—from the "New Plan" in the 1930s, to the Hutchins College of the 1940s, to the divisionally controlled College of the 1950s and 1960s, to the unified College curriculum of 1985 and its recent adjustments. General education has comprised 25 percent or 100 percent or 50 percent or 40 percent of an undergraduate's degree work here since 1929. The current curriculum, which was adopted by the faculty two years ago but which takes effect on your first day of classes, allocates your time among general education, electives, and your concentration almost equally.

I will have more to say about the theory underlying that structure in a few minutes, but for the moment, notice that the college curriculum has changed its structure radically over time. In every case, the changes have been fiercely contested. Indeed, the Hutchins College came into being only after a bitter fight and charges that the fundamental governance structure of the University had been manipulated in order to achieve the victory, which was secured by only one vote—that of the presiding officer, President Hutchins.[4] By contrast, curricular changes in the last two decades have proceeded on the basis of due deliberation, passed overwhelmingly, and adhered strictly to Roberts Rules of Order.

For many, the curriculum enjoys a mythic quality. But there are two myths apparently enjoying some lingering credence that must be corrected once and for all.

Myth One: *The general education curriculum is based on the "Great Books."* Several members of the faculty proposed in 1937 that the College curriculum be comprised solely of so-called great books, but the faculty rejected the proposal, so the losers decamped to Annapolis, Maryland, where they imposed their design on St. John's College. Our general education curriculum is built on original texts and fundamental questions, but it spans disciplines and genres. The goal is to pursue ideas, not to master specific tomes. (Here, I should add a parenthetical note about the Great Books. I am not hostile to the Great Books; indeed, I am a member of the board of directors of the Great Books Foundation. I think, however, that the pure Great Books curriculum fails, both as a full realization of liberal education and as a vehicle for improving society. Robert Maynard Hutchins thought that assiduous reading of the works approved by his compatriot, Mortimer Adler, would reveal truth and produce a "higher degree of social consensus." But as my colleague James Redfield, a loyal product of the Hutchins College, wrote several years ago: "[Hutchins] could think this only because his mind was working, not on the books, but on the interpretation of them; at his table one sat down with Plato and Kant, but one got up with Adler.")[5]

Now, Myth Two: *All wisdom resides in Hyde Park.* Until recently, concentration programs were structured such that junior years or terms abroad were barely feasible. There was an unspoken assumption among many of my colleagues that your I.Q. would drop fifty points if you left the neighborhood for educational purposes. That attitude is thankfully now obsolete. Our overseas programs are flourishing, especially our civilization sequences. The Core outside area code 773—a heresy until recently. (In fact, that has almost always been true to a limited extent. For example, no matter how ingenious our offerings may be in the natural sciences, you may be exempt from them if you satisfy established advanced-placement or other proficiency standards. In other words, you may have already satisfied part of your general education requirements, without even knowing it, at Lyons Township High School in La Grange, Illinois, or St. Agnes Academy in Houston, Texas.) The larger point is that our curriculum at some levels is a set of compromises between intellectual judgments and institutional imperatives. We may be confident and insistent, but we are not wholly impractical.

So much for lingering mythology. The heart of what we do here and what in my view accounts for whatever distinctive results we may enjoy has less to do with the number of courses or the precise configuration of subject matter than with the premises and standards of deliberation that inform our enterprise.

The fundamental goals of general education here were best expressed by Ronald Crane, who taught English, in 1931:

> [F]orming or developing what may be called basic intellectual habits—basic in the sense of being fundamental to all more advanced and specialized intellectual effort whether within the University or without. The ability to see problems, to define terms accurately and clearly, to analyze a question into its significant elements, to become aware of general assumptions and preconceptions upon which one's own thinking and that of others rests, to make relevant and useful distinctions, to weigh probabilities, to organize the results of one's own reflections and research, to read a book of whatever sort reflectively, analytically, critically, to write one's native language with clarity and distinction—the development of these powers . . . would seem to me to be no less the business of "General Education" than the communication and testing of knowledge, and I am not sure that they are not, in the long run, the most important and valuable fruits of a well-considered "General Education."[6]

In other words, Crane believed rightly that general education should be designed to establish an intellectual foundation in which skills and habits of mind were developed and honed. What we call the Core should encourage, by example and by practice, a cast of mind that is reflexively measured and deliberate, which weighs and responds rather than dogmatically proclaims.

"Example and practice" are essential components of the learning process which aims for Crane's results. But allow me to raise a caution flag. Charles Wegener, who has thought as hard as anyone in the University about what we are doing, has remarked, "It may be that all such teaching—from fly-fishing to laboratory science—amounts in the end merely to saying, 'Watch me; do what I do, and I promise you something interesting will happen.'"[7] The intertwined problem should be obvious, and is captured in the title of an essay on the art of teaching by our most famous fly-fisherman, Norman Maclean: "This Quarter I Am Taking McKeon."[8] When subject matter is reduced in the mind of the student to the intellectual style of an individual instructor, be it Richard McKeon or even Norman Maclean, the process of reflection has broken down. Or, as Wegener more elegantly puts it: "[M]ere imitation runs the serious risk of confusing the character of the activity with the way in which it is carried on by a particular person or persons—even, perhaps, a school or a tradition, whether of fly-fishing or physics."[9]

One neat solution to the problem was suggested several years ago by Grant Gilmore, the great commercial law teacher: "Great teachers should be taken out and shot at sunrise." There are solutions with lower transaction costs, of course. Indeed, the cure is to be reflective not only about substance but also about method. If you recognize that you are doing one type of literary analysis, you will simultaneously recognize that you have not exhausted the possibilities of the genre. That realization logically raises the possibility of other approaches. Anyone who insists that they have a corner on the ideal, in fly-fishing or in literary analysis, should be subjected to thoughtful skepticism, if not to Gilmore's brutal dictate.

Our obsessions here, especially in recent years, with core curricula have tended to obscure an earlier emphasis of general education, an emphasis loosely referred to as the "liberal arts." The term has been so abused in popular discourse that its principal function today is to distinguish what expensive American colleges and universities do from what technical or professional institutions do. The condescending implication of the usage seems to be irresistible to those in colleges and universities, at least until the question of vocation rears its ugly head. It is nonetheless worth considering for a minute what the liberal arts historically were meant to stand for and what relation they bear to the goals of general education that I have sketched.

Without quibbling too much over the difference between liberal arts and liberal education,[10] let me say that their ambition is liberation, that is, at least initially, to free men and women from dogma, comfortable choices, hasty conclusions, the confusion of sincerity for cogency, and all of the other features of slack thinking. But that is only the beginning. Habits of mind are in play whether you are reading *ESPN—The Magazine* or St. Augustine's *Confessions*. The value of the College is that you are encouraged to apply your capacities of mind to the most fundamental aspects of your life. As Charles Wegener has written: "[T]he liberal arts . . . are products of reflection upon activities in which we are already engaged. They are, to put it very directly, attempts to give some account of what we are doing and what we have done."[11] So, when Plato asks "What is justice?" or Kant asks "What can I know?" the inquiry resonates in all of us. The process of refining the question and developing the answer then unites the development of both habits of mind and their application to urgent questions that frame our entire lives. "Human beings," wrote Michael Oakeshott, "are what they understand themselves to be; they are composed entirely of beliefs about themselves and about the world they inhabit."[12] The function of education is to inform and discipline those beliefs. If, working together, we are successful, we will have initiated a process which carries past your baccalaureate convocation and which provides you with an intellectual apparatus for engaging your world. "What we are trying to do is never exhausted by what we actually do."[13] Speaking for myself, I can imagine no larger achievement than providing the means for an individual mind to interpret its own humanity in the world that it inherits.[14]

My brisk catalog of the components of liberal education, at least as I conceive of how it is practiced here, obviously lacks one very important factor, which might be called moral education. The topic is both so vast and so grave that under the circumstances I must deal with it quickly and somewhat facetiously. Secular institutions do not enjoy a comparative advantage in providing comprehensive moral education. In fact, the only academic curriculum of which I am aware, excluding church-controlled institutions, which addresses the issue directly was proposed, unsuccessfully, by dissenters to the "program" at St. John's. One tutor who escaped the Holocaust and thus felt the urgency for a syllabus of both moral and intellectual strenuousness, suggested this regimen:

> In the first year, students would read the Bible—both Old and New Testaments—and there would be daily beatings. In the second year, to demonstrate the limits of the human intellect, students would read Kant. In the third year, to show the human

> intellect gone astray, the text would be Hegel. In the final year, students would re-read the Bible, but there would be no beatings.

The curriculum obviously displays both coherence and risk, but none can doubt its integrity. I suspect it would be a non-starter here, although after five years at ground zero of curricular debates, I no longer make predictions on the issue.

Spirituality is not part of our curriculum in a prescriptive sense, nor is there a party line on public questions involving moral issues—although individual instructors certainly hold their own views. Everyone in the community, however, is committed to scholarly integrity and to intellectual honesty. Without fastidious treatment of sources and honest treatment of each other's positions, everything I say this afternoon would be a pious fraud. To say more on this point would insult your intelligence and the character that has brought you here.

So far, I have focused exclusively on general education, because that is the realm you will encounter first and because, as the Chief Justice lightly pointed out to Rachael, the Core has been "in the news." If you play your cards right, however, you will be finished with your general education requirements in two years, and you must elect your concentration and decide how to utilize your electives. I have less to say on these portions of your education, because they must seem achingly remote at this point and because their variety defies meaningful general treatment. In fact, the most I can confidently say at this point is this: Based on experience, at least 10 percent of you will concentrate in economics, 30 percent of you will at least begin as pre-med students, and 40 percent of you will change your concentration at least once.

The comparative advantage of a college located in a research university is both virtue and vice to the undergraduate. On the one hand, you can move immediately from general education and the introduction to disciplines to pre-professional and in some cases even graduate-level professional work. What could be more heady that advancing from the edge of a field to working with those men and women who are redefining it? The cultural racing change can be jarring—from generalist to mini-graduate student with the stroke of a pencil declaring what other colleges call a major. The risk is that you will consume the last two years of college absorbed exclusively in your concentration and even using electives as quasi-concentration courses to bulk up your portfolio.

At the risk of excommunication by my more professionally oriented colleagues, allow me to plant this thought in your mind for gestation in the fullness of time: no matter how consuming your concentration, approximately one-third of your course work here can be devoted to what are locally called "free electives." Some of you will spend advanced placement credit on your electives, perhaps to accelerate your graduation. Unless financially compelled, I think that would be a mistake. Electives are an opportunity to indulge the impulses of a dilettante without succumbing to the standards of a dilettante.

Put in different terms, which perhaps make the enterprise more worthy and reasonable, electives are an occasion to tailor your education to the person, in the exercise of growing maturity and responsibility, who you are choosing to become. "A human life is composed of performances," Oakeshott observed, "and each performance is a disclosure of a man's beliefs about himself and the world and an exploit of self-enactment. He is what he becomes; he has a history but no 'nature'. . . .

Human beings pursue satisfactions which they believe to be desirable, but human conduct is not the flowering of settled potentiality."[15] Remember the challenge at the end of Milton's *Paradise Lost*? "The world was all before them, where to choose / Their place of rest, and providence their guide: / They hand in hand with wandering steps and slow, / Through Eden took their solitary way."[16]

The elective provides the means for you to exercise self-definition, to develop taste and discernment if not authority, and to shape a life's attention. In vulgar terms this will be, for most of you, the last chance to receive expert tuition in what may be yearning curiosities or perhaps even the source of sustained leisure enjoyment from now until rigor mortis sets in. In many respects, the free elective provides a tailor-made liberal education in the second phase here of your undergraduate career and allows you to prevent your education from becoming another brick in your own wall.

What unites general education, specialized education, and what I have just re-cast as another form of liberal education is that all involve, indeed, consist of, acts of interpretation. The world does not come pre-packaged in units labeled "declining biodiversity," or "displaced aggression," or "Pareto-optimality." Describing, labeling, and measuring are all social acts committed with a deliberate purpose. The skills I referred to earlier provide the techniques for disciplining claims about what we observe. Those claims form the bases for interpretations, which generate arguments. If arguments are developed with care and discipline, then responsible judgments are possible. "*Education*," my colleague Jonathan Z. Smith says with italic emphasis, "*is argument about interpretations*."[17] Whether you are patiently developing an argument in the classroom or preparing the three-to-five-page essays which are central to the Hum and Soc cores, you are making a claim, identifying a thesis, substantiating your positions, anticipating counter-arguments, in short, offering—with energy and enthusiasm, I hope—*your* "take" on a problem deserving serious and sustained attention. Argument disciplined by these simple protocols is the life-blood of what we do.

Arguments here take place in an atmosphere variously described as "bracing,"[18] intense, or some other intimidating adjective. There is some truth to the refrain; our penchant for self-mythologizing is also in play. The terminology and protocols of debate are different from many academic institutions, beginning with the category you have unwittingly fallen into: you are first-year students, not freshmen. This is not an accommodation to political correctness; the terminology pre-dates the feminist revolution. (I have always thought it was a concession to what I hope is a vestige of the past—the implication that there might be fifth-, sixth-, seventh-year students, and so on. In all likelihood, the terms became fixed during the period when President Hutchins was trying to figure out whether higher education should begin with the eleventh or thirteenth grade.[19]) The most immediate tic of etiquette of which you should be aware is that professors are not called professors: they are referred to as "Mister," "Mrs.," or "Ms." The point is that good manners require decorum, not honorifics. (This is true everywhere, as far as I can tell, except in the Law School, and word apparently has not reached that distant shore.)

Once you know who you are and what to call your instructor, you are ready for what Hutchins insisted on calling the "great conversation" to begin. I will not tell you how to negotiate your classes. Nonetheless,

I can give you one inside tip: if you are stuck at the outset in the face of what seems to be a tenable but dubious claim, your reply should be, "But what's your evidence?" No rejoinder is more time-honored. It is the ultimate trump card, but it is most effective against the impetuous antagonist whose cart of convictions has gotten ahead of the horses of proof. If you decide to use the rejoinder, you need not raise your voice or employ any other histrionics: a good argument is its own amplification, and vehemence would be gratuitous and bad form.

Nor should you hesitate to raise fundamental questions. My colleague Rick Shweder even suggested on this occasion several years ago that you begin right away by arguing in your houses today that the Aims of Education Address "is nothing more than an arbitrary imposition of values by some power elite bent on preserving its privileges."[20] You may think that I am joking, but I am not (nor, I suspect, was Rick). If there is a cardinal feature of the ethos of our community, it is that no idea is off limits. David Daiches, the British literary critic, remarked that he was startled when he arrived on campus in the late 1930s that every feature of the educational program was being contested: "In Oxford it would have been bad taste to ask such fundamental questions, [but] in Chicago nothing was assumed, all questions were asked point blank, and you were not allowed to get away with a perfunctory answer."[21]

The attitude carries over, if anything with greater force, to intellectual claims about basic questions. Conventional wisdom is difficult to sustain if it is subject to chronic revalidation. In many social contexts, such incessant re-examination and "point-blank" debate would produce a cultural implosion. To the extent that we are largely free from that doleful feature that pervades so much of the academy, I think the reason is what might be called the "Godfather Morality." You may remember Sal Tessio's request to Tom Hagen as he was being taken away to pay the ultimate penalty for betraying the Corleones: "Tell Mike is wasn't personal, it was business."[22] So with argument here. Visitors from other institutions are struck by how little personal by-play transpires among colleagues here. In another place where I have taught, the ice-breaking question between colleagues was, "How 'bout those Redskins?" Anyone here who asks, "How 'bout those Bears?" would draw a blank stare, on principle, let alone on the merits. One final tip: if you are absolutely struck dumb during office hours with an instructor, ask, "What are you working on?" The question is the social equivalent of "What's your evidence?" during an argument. It, too, is time-honored, reflexively respected, but, for obvious reasons, it cannot be over-used.

No ethos can be captured in a snapshot or reduced to a signal incident, although every time I think of the themes we have explored today I think of a conversation several years ago at an annual event held at this time of year—the Transfer Students' Dinner (this year a luncheon). Every year, we enroll 100 or so transfer students from colleges and universities throughout the country. At our table, I was paired with the late Roger Weiss, who taught for many years in the Social Sciences Division and who seemed to embody the University's uncompromising commitment to intellectual standards and direct argument. Seated with us was a young man who was leaving a well-known eastern university after two years. He was bright, voluble, and eager to establish a rapport with faculty in his new digs—although that is not necessarily the point of the dinner. In any event, at one point Roger asked the man why he had transferred. The student delivered an extraordinarily revealing answer—one that immediately forced us to be confidantes as well as colleagues: "My philosophy teacher," he said. "He's also the president of the university, you know, and a real bully." I wanted to stop the story, for neither detail nor tone held promise, but the student forged ahead. "So one day in class, a dude asks a question, and you know what the professor says? You won't believe it, but he said: 'That is a stupid question which confirms that you have understood nothing today or all term.'" Our new colleague looked at both Roger and me, inviting if not begging for confirmation of his revulsion at the instructor's shocking behavior. I think in retrospect that the moment lasted only three or four seconds, but it seemed like minutes. I saw a social disaster gaping before me: the student sought solace or bonding or some other form of social intimacy. Unfortunately, he had mis-read his audience. Roger Weiss pulled himself up, somewhat more archly than necessary, and replied thoughtfully: "Well, *was* it a stupid question?"

If we—teacher and student—collectively do our jobs properly, in four years you will develop the taste to ask Roger's question, to have a firm foundation upon which to measure the answer, and to cherish an unremitting passion for the conversation.

Good luck and Godspeed. ❍

DENNIS J. HUTCHINSON, Professor in the College, Senior Lecturer in the Law School, and Master of the New Collegiate Division, delivered this address on September 19, 1999. This address is dedicated to Charles Wegener.

ENDNOTES

1. Compare Jonathan Z. Smith, "The Aims of Education [1982]," in John W. Boyer (ed.), *The Aims of Education* (Chicago: The University of Chicago, 1997), p. 230 (cited below as *Aims*).

2. F. Champion Ward, "Requiem for the Hutchins College," in John J. Macaloon (ed.), *General Education in the Social Sciences: Centennial Reflections on the College of the University of Chicago* (Chicago: The University of Chicago Press, 1992), pp. 77, 87.

3. John W. Boyer, *Three Views of Continuity and Change at the University of Chicago* (Chicago: The University of Chicago, 1999), p. 75.

4. William H. McNeill, *Hutchins' University: A Memoir of the University of Chicago, 1929–1950* (Chicago: The University of Chicago Press, 1991), p. 116 (cited below as "McNeill"). For another treatment of Hutchins and the College curriculum, see Edward Shils, "Robert Maynard Hutchins," in Joseph Epstein (ed.), *Portraits: A Gallery of Intellectuals* (Chicago: The University of Chicago Press, 1997), pp. 124, 132–36.

5. James Redfield, "Midway Dialogue: Robert Maynard Hutchins and His University," review of Harry S. Ashmore, *Unseasonable Truths: The Life and Times of Robert Maynard Hutchins*, in *Change*, May/June 1990, pp. 48, 50–51.

6. Quoted in Boyer, note 3 *supra*, at p. 52.

7. Charles Wegener, *Liberal Education and the Modern University* (Chicago: The University of Chicago Press, 1978), p. 93 (cited below as "Wegener").

8. Norman Maclean, " 'This Quarter I Am Taking McKeon': A Few Remarks on the Art of Teaching," in Ron McFarland and Hugh Nichols (eds.), *American Authors Series: Norman Maclean* (Lewiston, Idaho: Confluence Press), 1988, p. 57.

9. Wegener, p. 93.

10. Compare Leon R. Kass [1981], "The Aims of Liberal Education," in *Aims*, pp. 81, 86.

11. Wegener, p. 92.

12. Michael Oakeshott, "Education: The Engagement and Its Frustration," in Timothy Fuller (ed.), *The Voice of Liberal Learning: Michael Oakeshott on Education* (New Haven: Yale University Press, 1989), pp. 63, 64 (cited below as "Oakeshott").

13. Wegener, p. 64.

14. Compare Wegener, p. 95: "The problem of liberal education is to institutionalize those intellectual circumstances under which it is maximally probable that the reflective moment of intellectual activity will serve the purpose of permanently transforming the relationship of an individual mind to the intellectual world so that persons may become freely functioning participants in intellectual activity and autonomous members of the intellectual community."

15. Oakeshott, p. 64.

16. Book XII, ll. 647–50.

17. Smith, note 1 *supra*, at p. 226.

18. Hanna H. Gray [1987] in *Aims*, p. 63.

19. See Boyer, note 3 *supra*, at pp. 47–58, 67.

20. Richard A. Shweder [1993], "Fundamentalism for Highbrows," in *Aims*, pp. 191, 212.

21. McNeill at p. 88.

22. The line is rendered in the novel as, "Tell Mike it was business, I always liked him." Mario Puzo, *The Godfather* (New York: G. P. Putnam's Sons, 1969), p. 434.

jonathan lear

the aims of education address

2009

Students! Welcome to the University of Chicago. I am happy you are here, for you are a vital part of the life of the University. The University of Chicago is one of the great research universities in the world. Indeed, if one wrote a history of great institutions of advanced thinking and teaching, from Plato's Academy to the present, the University of Chicago would have to be in that account. There is no place I would rather be. The buildings are, of course, magnificent: not just the imposing grey stone and gothic architecture, but the somewhat dilapidated corridors and comfy cafes. The library is almost magical: you wish for a book and —poof!—it is in your hands. The administration is saavy and committed: it wants faculty and students to flourish. The lake is sublime: if you leave this chapel and take a left and walk straight out to the lake, then take another left and start walking northward towards the city center, you will find yourself walking a fine line between the sublime and the beautiful. On your right is this overwhelming lake, it is almost as long as England. Its colors—and thus its moods—change with the hours. But then straight ahead and on your left is the beauty of human creativity: the Chicago skyline is a museum of modern architecture. And in terms of the human, there is great music, great theater, great art, great coffee and great food, to be found all around us. We also live in Hyde Park, a wonderfully racially mixed neighborhood, full of unique vitality. Obviously, there have been problems, reflecting the national—and world-historical—blight that has been racism, and problems remain. That said, this is a real neighborhood. It is a place where people of all sorts of different backgrounds cherish being neighbors with each other. Living in this neighborhood one can learn a deeper meaning of civility. It is not, I think, an accident that the first African American President of the United States comes from our neighborhood. All of this adds significantly to the joy of being here, but it is not what makes the University great.

It is actually easy to say what does make this University great: conversation. In this community we not only have some of the best minds in the world—leading experts in virtually every field of inquiry—but we also value talking things out with each other. There is a shared understanding that if, in this brief time we are alive, we are going to figure out anything genuinely worthwhile, it will be through conversation. Each of our individual ideas needs to be tested against the countervailing thoughts of others; but even more important, it is the imagination of others that sparks our own. When I write an essay, the first dozen people I want to try it out on are colleagues here at the University. And by colleagues, I do not just mean fellow faculty members: I am indebted to the students I have worked with and have learned from their comments and criticism. The conversation transcends departments, divisions and schools. And it is utterly egalitarian in this sense: it does not matter what your age is, what your rank is, or where you have come from; all that matters is whether you can join a conversation that is trying to think out loud. This does not mean that anything goes, or that an idea is special just because you are. Learning how to think takes hard work, practice and patience. But it does mean that no idea is beyond question. Even the issue of how to think well is open to debate.

Enduring conversations about how things are—and how they might be—are as vulnerable as they are precious. I have seen universities where there are great minds but no conversation. This seems to me a living form of death, a university only in name. And once a conversation dies, it is all but impossible to get it started again: people go their own ways, pursuing their individual careers, and the whole becomes less than the sum of its parts. Even worse, I have witnessed conversations where there is pressure to conform to a particular point of view, as though right thinking requires agreement with current fashion. In the not-too-distant future, you will be sitting in a classroom, or on a student committee; you will hear the group coming to a consensus that you think is mistaken, and you will feel internal pressure to keep quiet. It is natural that you should feel this; the question is how you will act on it. Be warned: it is from such seemingly small moments that cowards are born. Plato, Aristotle and my wife, Professor Gabriel Lear, have taught me that one excellent reason for not acting in a cowardly way is that if you do so, you are likely to become a coward. From such moments character is built. (Similarly, one excellent reason not to cheat is that, if you do cheat, you are likely to become a cheater.)

I said earlier that you are a vital part of the life of the University. We can now see what that means: you play a crucial role in keeping this precious conversation alive. One might at first think: Why should a great research university have an undergraduate college at all? Why not let great minds do their research unencumbered by teaching? And why not let undergraduates be taught by teachers who may not be that good at research, but are good at explaining the accumulated wisdom of the ages?

The University of Chicago is committed in its very being to the thought that such a partition does not ultimately work. Professors need to be brought back to the open, questioning minds of those who do not yet know what we purportedly do know. We need to be able to explain ourselves. You have a way of keeping us honest and open, of reminding us of what we do and do not know. It is, quite literally, refreshing. I am going to be teaching in the Human Being and Citizen core this quarter, and I expect to learn from my students and revise my opinions about what is involved in being a human being and a citizen. I expect some of you will teach me to read a passage differently in books that I have read and re-read throughout my adult life. Conversely, a great undergraduate teacher is someone who not only has a love for the accumulated attempts of human beings to figure out what is true or to grasp something beautiful, but also has a healthy suspicion of anything that tries to pass itself off as "accumulated wisdom". The healthiest form of suspicion is to be found in the active researcher, who has a lively sense of how much she or he does not know. Welcoming undergraduates into a great university and having its professors teach at all levels is its own form of truthfulness.

Some of you may feel you have come to just the right place, but others may feel a bit overwhelmed. I would like to offer a word of reassurance. I have been teaching for decades, and all that time I have been looking for a special student I have not yet found. That special student is the one who will write a first undergraduate paper that is even worse than the one I wrote when I entered university. I can still vividly remember going to see the professor—believe me, *not* to complain about the grade, but because *he* asked to see me. He had the delicacy of an ambulance driver who has just arrived at a bad accident. He just wanted to know: *How did this ever happen?!* To say that I wrote a very bad paper is to give me too much credit. I don't think one should call what I wrote *a* paper. It did not have enough unity for that. You might think this meeting must have been an excruciating embarrassment, but it actually came as a relief—an even greater relief than that dawning moment in tenth grade when I realized, two months into the course, that *plane* geometry was not a precursor for *fancy* geometry (whatever that is), but was actually the study of spatial figures on a plane surface. The meeting with the professor was a relief because I did have an inkling that I was lost, and for a professor to recognize that I was lost helped me to get my bearings. At last I knew where I was: I was lost! The professor gave me this advice: When you write a paper, do not write what you think you are supposed to write. Instead, read the book and take time to think about it. If you are asked a question, think about what the question is really asking and then try to answer it as clearly as you can. This simple advice has helped me ever since.

By the way, if you think professors are assigning too much reading for you to take the time to think, you should say something about it. Talk to your professor or bring it up as an issue in class. This is important. One way a conversation dies at a university is if professors assign too much reading. Students then feel the need to skim or grab clichés off the internet and, instead of a real conversation, students and faculty trade slogans. Everyone can say they have read the books when in fact no one has. On *Saturday Night Live*, there used to be a character, Father Guido Sarducci, who offered to teach you everything you would learn at college—and remember five years later. Tuition was twenty bucks, money-back guaranteed. I suppose with Plato's *Republic* one might remember it had something to do with a cave. The reason I teach that book in a course that is entirely devoted to it—taking up an entire quarter—is that I do not think you can even be introduced to the book, you certainly cannot read it, unless you are willing to devote that kind of time and thinking to it. I want every course I teach to be one where Father Sarducci would have to refund the money he charged—*not* because you have remembered lots of facts, but because you have learned how to read. He could never teach that.

When Dean Boyer invited me to give this Aims of Education Address, my first thought was suspicious: what is the *s* doing in the title? Why isn't there a single aim that education has? Obviously, there are many things we are trying to do here at the University, and many values we can articulate. But is there not also one overarching aim—that encompasses these diverse projects and ideals, that is *the* aim of education? And if there is one *s*, why aren't there two: the aim*s* of education*s*? If there is not one overarching aim, why think there is a single activity—education—as opposed to a plurality of educations, each fulfilling its own aim? The University would then be a kind of holding company—perhaps a physical location where all these different educations happen to occur. I was suspicious that the *s* might be covering over laziness. After all, if there is nothing more to say than that there are multiple aims, then year after year a speaker can get up and talk about an aim of education without any sense that he or she might be in conflict with past or future speakers, without any sense that there is a problem that still needs to be worked out. The assumption would be that people are simply speaking about different aims.

I wrote to the Dean, who is a distinguished historian of this institution, to ask if he knew how this annual lecture acquired its title. His answer is too long to recount! But the title goes back to a lecture that the philosopher and mathematician Albert North Whitehead delivered to the British Mathematical Association as his Presidential Address in 1916. When I read Whitehead's lecture this summer, I became convinced that *he* gave it the wrong title for there is only one aim that he puts forward. Whitehead is aware that he is speaking in the midst of World War I which he calls a "crisis in European civilization". But even more than the threat of German guns, he is worried about the effect of teachers on the next generation. Here is a quote from his address that still ring true:

> Culture is activity of thought, and receptiveness to beauty and humane feeling. Scraps of information have nothing to do with it. A merely well-informed man is the most useless bore on God's earth. . . . In training a child to activity of thought, above all things we must beware of what I will call "inert ideas"— that is to say, ideas that are merely received into the mind without being utilized, or tested, or thrown into fresh combinations. In the history of education, the most striking phenomenon is that schools of learning, which at one epoch are alive with a ferment of genius, in a succeeding generation exhibit merely pedantry and routine. The reason is that they are overladen with inert ideas. Education with inert ideas is not only useless: it is above all things harmful. . . . The solution which I am urging is to eradicate the fatal disconnection of subjects which kills the vitality of our modern curriculum. *There is only one subject-matter for education, and that is Life in all its manifestations.*

Our curriculum is in much better shape than the one Whitehead deplored. But the way I would put the basic point he is making is this: *the* aim of education is to teach us how to be students.

By *student* I do not mean a member of the socially recognized category: those people, like yourselves, who are enrolled in a social institution, a school or university. Rather, a *student* in the deeper sense is a category of human being. A student in this deeper sense is a person committed to holding him- or herself open to the lessons the world has to teach. To put it mildly, this is not as easy as it might at first sound. For "holding oneself open" is not some vague good feeling about being in the world. It regularly requires enormous hard work and self-discipline: rigorously adhering to methods of inquiry that the world has taught us is the way to ask it questions; sometimes it requires us to question and re-think those very methods of inquiry; and sometimes we are required to adjust the way we see the world and to adjust the way we live. On occasion that is painful: we are forced to recognize that beliefs that matter to us are unjustified; indeed, that we have held them through some combination of complacency, arrogance and prejudice. By "the world" I do not mean just learning from nature but also from other people living in the world, along with their creations. There is no end to the process of forming ourselves into people who are genuinely open to what the world has to teach us. Becoming a student in this deeper sense is a life-task. Part of what it is to *be* a student is to be forever in the process of *becoming* one.

It seems to me that this is the form that human flourishing takes—though it has infinite variations. For it is given to us in our very nature that we are not gods. We are not omnipotent beings nor are we omniscient.

It is built into our situation that we inhabit an environment upon which we depend for our very existence—and certainly for our happiness—but over which we have limited control and imperfect understanding. This is not just a fact that happens to be true of us it is the structure of our very being. Some of our vulnerabilities are obvious: individually, we might get hurt or injured, our loved ones may die, and at some point each of us is going to die; collectively, we might starve, be wiped out or wipe each other out. Other vulnerabilities are harder to spot, but just as important: great scientific and social revolutions have taught us, through painful disruptions, that the very concepts with which we think may break down as we attempt to understand ourselves and the world.

To be or become a student is basically to say *hooray!* to all of that. It is to embrace our inevitably limited, vulnerable condition by committing ourselves to being open to learning what we do not yet understand. And that includes revising the concepts with which we try to understand. Thus being a student manifests astonishing hopefulness. In my writing I have called it *radical* hope because, unlike ordinary cases, we cannot say in any detail what we are hoping for. And we need not be self-consciously hoping for anything. But the hope is there, manifest in the very activity of reaching out to the world to try to understand it. To put it in broad, if somewhat enigmatic, terms: In trying to undertand the world we inhabit, we manifest the hope that the world will show itself to be intelligible to the best efforts of finite, fallible creatures like ourselves. Why, after all, should the world be intelligible to the human mind? Why, when we inquire, do things start to hang together in intelligible wholes, rather than falling apart into a disparate, incomprehensible mess? And why, when things do not hang together, do we keep looking for ways they might? One could teach a course in the history of philosophy organized around the different attempts to answer these questions. I still have not found answers I find satisfying.

So in all seriousness I can say that if you make really good use of your time here at the University and if we do a really good job of educating you, by the time you graduate you will be ready to become a student. We will try to help you develop into a person who is *good at* examining and learning from the world, other people, and your own experience. *That* is the aim of education.

Being a student in this deeper sense is, I think, to inhabit the realm of human freedom and human happiness. Anything else that puts itself forward as a candidate—wealth or pleasure, power or recognition and honor—either gets its plausibility because it can be integrated into a life that is genuinely holding itself open and in so doing provides an added bloom to that life, or it is a false appearance. It is one thing to incorporate these goods into a life that is holding itself open to learning, but it is a true disaster to give up a life of learning in order to obtain one of these other purported goods. I am not saying anything about social professions. There are infinite ways one can hold oneself open in life. One can be a student in this deeper sense while occupying all manner of social roles; conversely, one can occupy the social role of student (or teacher) and be dead as a doornail.

Let me put in a word for the humanities. My education is primarily in philosophy which is a humanities discipline. If I were a scientist or a social scientist, I would be giving a different lecture. What fills me with admiration for scientists and social scientists is the way they are able to ask bold questions while at the same time holding themselves to strict and widely agreed-upon norms of inquiry. Of course, one can argue about the norms—that too is part of the conversation. And sometimes agreed-upon norms are disturbed or even overturned. But to be someone who can direct her inquiries into nature (or human nature) and all the while constrain herself to strict norms of inquiry that not only the scientific community but she herself endorses: *that* is a truly remarkable answer to the question, What is it to be a student of nature? And it shows that *scientist* is an ethical category: for one is freely choosing to live according to strict norms of inquiry in community with other scientists and as a member of the larger social world.

But when it comes to the humanities, what entrances me is their ability to open up the deepest questions where we had previously thought everything was obvious. For example, being a student: there really is no bottom to the question, What is it to be a person who can hold himself open to what can be learned from the world? Even after we have measured everything we can measure in nature and in the human world, there are still going to be questions: What is it to hold oneself open? What is it to be a person? What is it to learn something? What do we mean by "the world": is the world another thing? And if not, what is it? To let the humanities enter your soul is to realize that these are not just theoretical questions, from which one can stand back and inquire in a disinterested way. The questions have not really been heard unless they start to strike you in the first person and demand from you answers that consist not just in papers you write, but in practical decisions about how you are going to live. In trying to figure out what it is to hold oneself open, one is naturally led to study the myriad attempts humans have made over time to open themselves to the world's lessons. I take it that many of the great works of literature, history and the visual arts are inquiries into what such openness ultimately is. But these great works have not reached their target unless for some *I*, it grabs *me*. Not just as an item of aesthetic interest, but as a confrontation with the way I live.

I would not need to be telling you all this if there were not something in our character that pulls us away from becoming a student. In the very first line of the *Metaphysics,* Aristotle says, "All humans by their nature desire to understand."[1] But history has taught us that we human beings also have a desire not to know. In peculiar but characteristic ways, we are motivated to hold onto our ignorance—though that is never how it seems to us at the time. It marks us as human that we both desire to know and are motivated not to know. In December 1784, the philosopher Immanuel Kant published in the *Berlinische Monatsschrift* "An Answer to the Question: What Is Enlightenment?" As the title suggests, it was a response to a question that had previously been posed in the magazine. The first paragraph is stunning in its confrontation:

> Enlightenment is the human being's emergence from his *self-imposed* immaturity. Immaturity is inability to make use of one's own understanding without direction from another. This immaturity is *self-imposed* when its cause lies not in lack of understanding but in lack of resolution and courage to use it without direction from another. *Sapere aude!* Have courage to make use of your *own* understanding!: that is the practical saying of enlightenment.

I find this statement both unignorable and confusing. There are two imperatives: "*Sapere aude!*"—normally translated as "Dare to know!" but it could also be understood as "Have the audacity to understand!"—and "[M]ake use of your *own* understanding!" But if Kant wants us to think for ourselves, why is he telling us what to do? Why should we take *his* word for it? Presumably, we need to think for ourselves why it is a good idea to think for ourselves. I think we should hear these imperatives not as orders coming from Kant, but rather as a *direct address*: Kant wants to "get in our face"—that is what "confront" means—like an insistent beggar who will not let us walk by without facing up to the fact that that is what we are doing. It is not an order; it is a challenge. If Kant is right that it takes resolution and courage to think for yourself, we must be creatures who tend toward childishness. For courage and resoluteness are remarkable human qualities: One does not find them often among humans. We seem to be creatures who want to follow along, to take other people's word for it. This is the immaturity that Kant says is self-imposed—and it is not at all correlated with biological age. He thinks it takes courage and steadfastness to think, to inquire, to come to understand something. Why should that be?

As for why it takes courage, I think the answer is that *every* time you try to think something through for yourself—no matter how trivial-seeming or obvious—you risk alienating your own community. That is, there is at least a chance that you will come up with a different answer from the settled opinions of your neighbors; and there is also a chance that, instead of honoring you for expanding the scope of our shared understanding, the community will be irritated with you for rocking the boat—and will seek to bully you, ridicule you, ostracize you or worse.

So to understand the courage required for thinking, one must also take a sober look at the *lack* of courage that is so common in human life. Let us consider what happened to the best student in the history of the world—at least my candidate for that title. He was condemned to death by a majority vote of those fellow citizens who participated on the jury. How could that have happened? It is uncanny for me to be talking to you about Socrates, for I first read Plato's *Apology* when I was your age. Little did I know then that I would be reading this text countless times throughout my life. But when I read it now what sticks out is different than what bothered me then. Back then I was struck by the pathos of the situation: that a majority of jurors would vote for the death of one of the finest human beings who ever lived. What stands out now is that, in an important sense, *no one* voted for his death.

In the *Apology*, Socrates says that much more formidable than the explicit charges against him are the rumor and slander that people have been hearing about him since childhood.[2] These are rumors that get hold of us in our genuine immaturity, before we are able to examine them. And by the time we are able to examine them, they are already structuring our outlook. As a result, Socrates says that when it comes to his defense, he is forced to "fight with shadows" and to "cross-examine when no one answers".[3] He gives an account of how these rumors arose—as if a genealogy of falsehood might free the jurors from their haze of prejudice. As a student, he questioned people who claimed to have knowledge—and he repeatedly came up empty. In their injured pride they accused him of "corrupting the youth," but, Socrates says, "If one asks them what he [Socrates] does and what he teaches to corrupt them, *they are silent, as they do not know*".[4] Instead they throw out clichés about philosophers that are patently not true of Socrates. And then Socrates utters a sentence I used to pass over, but now has become the most haunting line of the text: "If you look into this either now or later, this is what you will find".[5] That is, Socrates tells the jurors that if they will only consider the matter, they will see for themselves that the charges against him are baseless. So if a disagreement does persist, it must be because some are actively refusing to think things through for themselves. In Kant's terms, they are insisting on their immaturity. But children cannot vote. In an important sense, there is no one there making up his mind. Rather, there is only a childish going along with rumors—the "shadows" where "no one answers".

In his cross-examination of Meletus, the person who is officially bringing the charges against him, Socrates shows with devastating clarity that Meletus is only mouthing clichés that he does not understand and cannot defend. Nor can anyone else. And so Socrates is put to death in spite of the fact that, in an important sense, no one has really made a charge against him (that is, there is no substantial charge), no one really understands what the charge is, no one has any evidence for the charge, and those who are inclined to vote in favor are motivated not to understand the situation which, if they chose, they could easily understand and which they are called upon to judge.

This, I suspect, is what horrified Plato: not Socrates' death per se, but the motivated ignorance that led to it. And what is truly horrifying is the thought that this is not simply a tragic historical moment, but that motivation towards ignorance is pervasive in human life: that it is present in each of us and marks us as human. On reflection, it is not surprising that this should be so. For it goes to the heart of the human condition that none of us is in a position to make up our minds about absolutely everything and we must inevitably rely on the judgment of others, as well as on the accumulated wisdom of society. For some things we must take other people's word for it: and in some respects this is a very good thing, building community and common purpose, as well as extending our knowledge far beyond what any individual could achieve. It is obviously an evolutionary advantage that we share our knowledge. But this also creates a vulnerability: precisely because we rely so heavily on our community to provide an orientation, we often do not know whether what we are relying on really is knowledge or accumulated prejudice and unquestioned assumptions. And, strange as it may seem at first, it makes sense that we should be motivated not to find out the difference: for the whole package of knowledge and assumption provides an orientation to the world on which the community has been relying. It can feel threatening to a whole way of life to question any part of it. The problem is intensified by the fact that society tends to reward people who are good at telling us what we already purportedly know, and we have been selected so as to care about winning society's recognition. Thus there are powerful forces, within us and around us, that motivate us not to question the received wisdom of the moment. Luckily for us, this is not the only motivation we have, but we are motivated to stick with what we purportedly already know.

That is why it takes courage to think. The point is *not* that everyone around you is a herd animal relying on prejudice and that when you think you will inevitably alienate yourself from the group. Often, when you think you will come to discover for yourself that the received wisdom is indeed wisdom. And on many occasions when you think for yourself you will be honored and rewarded by society. Good things often happen. The point is rather that every time you think you risk the *possibility* that you are going to come up with an answer that puts you out on a limb, and as you attempt to think again you only end up further out on that limb. That possibility may not actually come to fruition in your life, but it will be there *as a possibility* every time you try to think a problem through.

That is why the conversation at the University of Chicago is so precious. At its best, it is a community that encourages us to be courageous: to think a problem through precisely because it is worth thinking it through. This capacity for thinking also marks us as human, and it is well worth supporting. I am told that in Lake Wobegon, "all the women are strong, all the men are good-looking, and all the children are above average." I cannot tell you how happy I am that I live at the edge of a different lake! Our students are certainly not all above average, and I don't even know what it means to say they—you—are all outstanding. What I hope is that each of you is willing to take on the risk of trying to think something through. That is, each of you is willing to take on the risk of becoming an oddball. Let me be clear: I do not think there is anything valuable about being an oddball as such. It is thinking that matters, as well as living in the light of one's thinking. The courage Kant is talking about is in recognizing that when you think a problem through it is at least possible you will find yourself on the other side of an established consensus. You can then try to convince others with your reasons: sometimes that will work; other times others will help you to see reasons you have overlooked, reasons that support established opinion. But if thinking does lead us to an unusual position, so be it. This is no more than saying that at the edge of our lake we live in a community where our students are students.

But if you are going to take on this challenge to become a student, you have to take on another: how are you at one and the same time going to think for yourself and *submit* yourself to the teaching that the University of Chicago has to offer? This is a difficult question: for you both have to make up your own mind about what to learn and whether a proposed course of learning really does help you in your own attempts to develop, *and*, at least provisionally and up to a point, you have to take other people's word for what learning consists in. How does one walk this tightrope? This is a question that confronts you directly, and you have only four years to answer it. Speaking for myself, I made poor use of my freedom when I was in college: I used it to avoid educational challenges that would have helped me to grow. And I lacked the maturity to see what I was doing. This time I offer my failure not as consolation, but as a warning. I was lucky enough to be offered a chance to do a second B.A. degree at a university abroad, and the second time around I made better choices. If I had not had that chance, my life would have taken a significantly different course, and I do not think it would have been for the better. So the decisions you make now do matter, and it is perfectly possible for you to make important bad decisions. I wish there were a way to protect you from this, but the alternatives are even worse.

The obvious alternative is for us teachers to direct your studies even more than we already do. Actually, we are such a contentious lot that it is unlikely we could agree on any such course. But that is for the good. It is a culturally significant fact that when Professor Whitehead gave his

Aims of Education Address, he was speaking to teachers, whereas the Aims of Education Address at the University of Chicago is addressed to students. Again, one might at first think that if the lecture really is about the aims of education, it ought to be directed to teachers who themselves need to learn how to teach. But if the aim of education is to teach you how to become and be a student, then I've got the better audience. It is constitutive of teaching openness to inquiry that you, the students, should be granted serious conversational partnership in what that openness consists in. That does not mean that I think your judgment is as good as mine. For many educational issues, I do not think it is. But it does mean that for a wide range of issues neither I nor anyone else has the power to require anything of you: the most we can do is offer our reasons for thinking that a particular course of study is a good or a bad idea. It is up to you to exercise your reason and decide whether the reasons we have given you are good or not. We, of course, may criticize your choices, but again we have to give our reasons, and again you must decide what you think of them. This is what it is to teach openness—or, at least, it is one crucial ingredient—and it is what Kant called enlightenment, the leaving of one's childish practices behind. But the fact that we teach people to make important, life-shaping decisions by treating them as though they are already capable of make such decisions is a serious business, fraught with dangerous missteps.

It is not an accident that the words "dogma" and "dogmatic" have become pejorative terms. The ancient Greek word *dogma* comes from the verb *dokéō* (to seem), and it meant opinion, belief, decision and judgment. It came to mean a received body of principles or a doctrine. I hope you can spend a moment to conjure up the heart-wrenching aspect of our predicament. Dogma in the original sense is the accumulated wisdom of the ages. It is that learning which one generation has to pass on to the next. And no civilization is stronger than the link between generations. If a civilization cannot pass on its wisdom, it is over. If only one could *simply* pass on the dogma of an age. As it turns out, that is not possible: dogma inevitably becomes dogmatic, and one ends up murdering the learning that one is trying to pass along.

So, the decisions about how to become and be a student are significantly in your hands, though we are here to help. I hope I have said enough to make it clear that Kant was not kidding when he said it took courage. Let me give you three concrete pieces of advice. First, go talk to your professors in their office hours: not to impress them or curry favor, but for conversation about the issues that matter to you. I have found that conversations I had with my professors continue to resonate with me decades later. Second, take risks. I have said that the decisions you make now matter, but you have completely misunderstood me if you conclude that you should be very cautious in the courses you take. *That* is a prime example of the bad decision that matters. You should be trying out courses that stretch you, that do not come easily, that open up realms of inquiry that are at the moment closed to you. Above all, do not become a slave to your resumé. That is no way to live. When I sit on an admissions committee I am much more impressed with the student who got lower grades because she stretched herself to take a wide range of challenging courses than with the student who aced a familiar field. Third, be on guard for moments in our own university life where our conversation is unwittingly disrupted by gossip, rumor and conventional wisdom. This can happen in seemingly small moments. Let me give you an example with which you may well disagree. At the end of every quarter, students are encouraged—I believe by the Dean's Office—to fill out an online questionnaire evaluating the courses they have taken and the professors who taught them. I warn my students that filling out that questionnaire is dangerous; they are taking their lives in their hands. It is not that I am opposed to students evaluating teachers; quite the opposite. And I am also in favor of transparency: that student evaluations should be open for all to consult. But why is this initiative coming from the Dean's Office rather than *from you,* the students? And why is the Dean's Office responsible for setting up the form of the evaluation—why does it take the form of a questionnaire, rather than some other form? And why aren't you the students deciding what form it should take? My worry is that tacitly—without anyone quite realizing it—you are being taught that you are consumers. It is as though education is a product you can purchase and courses are commodities. Just as I regularly get an online questionnaire from a car rental company or a hotel after I have used their services, so you too can register customer satisfaction or dissatisfaction. I think this misleads you about who you are and what you are doing. To teach you that your relation to education is basically one of consumption is, I think, a grievous misunderstanding.

But don't take my word for it! The important point is not whether you agree with me, but whether you are willing to think for yourselves about what it is to be a student and not simply accept the established routines as already providing the answer. This takes resoluteness, that other term Kant used alongside courage. What does it mean? I think he is referring to the steadfastness required to think a problem through, the sustained hard work involved in getting things right, rather than settling for a cliché, a hunch or received opinion. And he is also referring to the resolve to revise one's beliefs or even give them up altogether if they cannot stand up to scrutiny. At the beginning of his *History of the Peloponnesian War*—and if you want to know about the human condition, this is one of the best books ever written—Thucydides writes of the effort involved in constructing his narrative. He was not willing to settle for the first accounts he received of an important event or battle; nor was he willing to trust even own impressions. He recognized that even eye witnesses have faulty memories, and their sincere accounts might be skewed because they favored one side or another. So he tested the alternative accounts against each other, subjecting each report to "the most severe and detailed tests possible". This, Thucydides tells us, was hard work. The result, he says, is not a romantic tale, but an accurate account of what happened for those in the future who would like to know about it. He concludes with a line that, from the perspective of two-and-a-half-thousand years, packs a wallop: "I have written my work, not as an essay which is to win the applause of the moment, but as a possession for all time." Now *that* is resoluteness. He is willing to give up on recognition and honor in his own lifetime—he even dismisses it by calling it "the applause of the moment"—because he is committed to the idea that accuracy, getting things right, about this important historical event will have its own enduring power. Was he right about that? I do not think the answer is at all obvious—in spite of the fact that we are still reading it and learning from it. Again, this is something *you* need to think about. What is it for something to be a possession for all time?

I am reminded of something the philosopher Bernard Williams

wrote close to the end of this life. Williams was my teacher when I first started to study philosophy; later he became my colleague and friend, and we taught seminars together. He was awarded an honorary doctorate here at the University of Chicago. Williams wrote:

> Nietzsche . . . got it right when he said that once upon a time there was a star in the corner of the universe, and a planet circling that star, and on it some clever creatures who invented knowledge; and then they died and the star went out and it was as though nothing had happened.[6]

What then of Thucydides' aspiration to create a possession for *all* time? Do we want to say that Thucydides got it wrong: that his book only lasted for a short time, and the universe then went on without it? Or do we want to say that Thucydides' history was a possession for all time, but time itself ran out? These are difficult questions, and I am without an argument or a confident thought on the matter. But I do have an intuition. My intuition is that Thucydides did create a possession for all time. If the universe should come to be a place where that is no longer apparent, then that is a terrible loss for the universe, but Thucydides was on the right track. Think about it: what would it be for the universe to look *as though* truly great things had happened—the creation of possessions for all time, the creation of beauty, and the discovery of significant truths, as well as the performance of good acts? What would it be for the universe to appear *as though* these things *had* happened before *it* ran out of steam? It would look exactly the same way. As I said, I do not yet have an argument. But, if you are interested, we are lucky enough to be in an institution where we can talk about this over time. So let me close with the words with which I began, though I hope by now they have a deeper resonance: Students! Welcome to the University of Chicago. ❍

JONATHAN LEAR, the John U. Nef Distinguished Service Professor in the John U. Nef Committee on Social Thought, the Department of Philosophy, and the College, delivered this address on September 24, 2009.

ENDNOTES

1. Aristotle, *Metaphysics* I.980a21.

2. Plato, *Apology* 18b.

3. Ibid. 18d.

4. Ibid. 23d.

5. Ibid. 24a–b.

6. Bernard Williams, *Philosophy As a Humanistic Discipline,* p. 138. The original quote comes from Friedrich Nietzsche, "On Truth and Lies in a Non-Moral Sense."

tanya luhrmann

the aims of education address

2003

When I was an undergraduate I went in my first days as a freshman, to my own college's version of the Aims of Education address. The talk was no doubt meant to introduce me to the university and to persuade me to take the right attitude towards my studies. I had arrived in the autumn of 1976, in the aftermath of a glorious celebration of our nation's bicentennial. The fireworks had been particularly splendid that July. Hundreds of tall ships like those used in the revolutionary era sailed up the east coast in a triumphant reenactment of the past. Tea was dumped into Boston harbor. People wore festive hats. 1976 was also the aftermath of the less glorious Vietnam war and the great social upheaval that had turned society upside down. Race, class, and (most recently) gender were no longer supposed to define the roles people chose to play at work or at home. This turned out to be an illusion, of course, but only partly an illusion. People who came of age with my generation had possibilities before them that were simply unthinkable in earlier times. I was part of a brave new world in which I and my classmates could simply choose to be whatever and whoever we wanted to be. This filled us with terror.

I remember being at that talk and looking around at all the people. I remember how large the auditorium was, and how small the lecturer looked, how far away he was from me, and I remember what it felt like to be sitting there, one nervous excited person among a vastness of other people. Four years seemed like an eternity. Even though I had picked out my courses and chosen a major, I remember even now how uncertain I was about everything and about how it would all turn out. Unfortunately, I can't remember a single word of the lecture. This does raise the question of what we are doing here today. But it also suggests to me how I can be most helpful, by talking about why you are anxious and uncertain, as I expect you are, and why a liberal education will help you to cope.

These are the years of your greatest confidence and your greatest insecurity. To borrow from a famous pen, for you these are the best of times and the worst of times—because of the era in which we live, because of the place and class in which we are located, and because of your age, your point, as it were, of development. You are not bound by many obvious external limitations. Simply by being here, you establish your place in the middle class. Last year the Aims address was delivered by a member of the university's sociology department, Andy Abbott, who garnered the data from recent graduating classes and figured out that those who graduate from this university end up taking jobs that place them well within the upper income brackets in this country. It doesn't matter what major you choose. It doesn't even matter what grades you get. If the economy of the near future is anything at all like the economy of the near past, you will do well in life, at least materially. The real uncertainty is not whether you will succeed economically, but how you will choose to do it—what you will actually do. You have before you all the wonderful possibilities of who you can become, an infinitude of possible selves. This is a wonderful opportunity and a terrible, nearly unbearable, burden.

At the beginning of the twentieth century, the anthropologist Margaret Mead wrote an ethnography about your stage of life, called *Coming of Age in Samoa.* She spent nine months on a palm-strewn island in the

South Pacific hanging out with adolescent girls, and she wrote in her famous book that these girls came to adulthood relatively untroubled by the emotional storms and generational conflicts of American adolescents. The book became famous because Mead suggested, in 1928, that a little hands-on experience with sex was good for young people. (She also thought that a little hands-on experience with death and corpses was good for them, but somehow, American parents found that point less interesting.) Mead drew a most compelling picture of paradise. Here she describes the end of a village day:

> Girls gather flowers to weave into necklaces; children, lusty from their naps and bound to no particular task, play circular games in the half shade of the late afternoon. Finally the sun sets, in a flame which stretches from the mountain behind to the horizon on the sea, the last bather comes up from the beach, children straggle home, dark little figures etched against the sky; lights shine in the houses, and each household gathers for its evening meal . . . Sometimes sleep will not descend upon the village until long past midnight; then at last there is only the mellow thunder of the reef and the whisper of lovers, as the village rests until dawn (pp. 18–19).

Some years later, another anthropologist went back to the community and reported that the villagers were outraged by these slanderous tales of easy, untroubled sex among the young people. Mead had spoken to the young women; this new anthropologist spoke to the fathers, and the difference in their accounts was a bit like the difference between what you might tell a friend about a party you'd attended and what your parents might say if the University of Chicago admissions counselor had asked them, at the interview, for a description of your after-school activities.

In any event, the conclusions Mead drew still ring true. She pointed out that in a place like Samoa, where social roles are clear and for the most part prescribed by tradition, the emotional challenge of adulthood is very different than in our own. Young men and women in the Samoan village of Mead's fieldwork come to adulthood with a very clear idea of what they will do in the years ahead. They will fish and cultivate taro in the fields; they will live in huts thatched with palm and floored with stone; they will tend the younger children; and then as their children age, their older children will tend the younger babies. Men and women have different tasks, and those tasks are well understood. The burden of cooking falls upon women and the burden of planting, house building, and fishing upon the men, though each to some extent will learn the skills of both. Women also are the weavers, and the worth of a girl can be seen partly in the quality of the mats and baskets and blinds she weaves from the ever-present palm fronds she must gather. She does not aim to be the best weaver on the island; for her there are no rewards for unbridled excellence. She just needs to be good enough. The boys have a harder time in Samoa. Senior men will give some of them, as they age, the right to sit in assembly with community leaders, to drink ceremonial kava with them, and to have status and authority in their village, and the competition to be chosen is fierce and subtle. But all men and women know the faith they will follow, all know the means by which they will gain their living, and all know the people with whom they will pass their lives.

You know none of that. You enter into adulthood—and these four years of college are really your transition into adulthood—with more choice than the world has ever known. Take, for example, what it is to be female. About half of you are female. Some of you see your future selves as defined by your intellectual work. You imagine that work to be your first commitment. If it so happens that you never have children or never even marry, that will be okay in the eyes of your peers. There will be many women like you at your twentieth reunion. Others of you who are female see your future selves as primarily mothers and wives. You imagine your yet-to-be-born children as your first commitment, and if you never have much of a professional career, that too will be okay in the eyes of your peers. There will also be many women like you at the twentieth reunion. If you are a middle-class woman in our society it's okay to be a stay-at-home mom, or a childless professional, or to balance both career and family. For that matter, it's okay to go to a sperm bank and have a kid on your own or even with another woman. I went to college in an era when for the first time it was possible and widely acceptable for women to delay pregnancy so that they could decide whether and when to have a child and when, again for the first time, deciding to go to graduate school had become a normal and acceptable choice for women. Now, the barriers have fallen even further. There are fewer prejudices about women in traditionally male-dominated fields and fewer presumptions about how and when to raise a family. None of you will be as constrained as previous generations were by gender, by sexual orientation, by skin color, by the class status of your parents, nor even by your accent or the language of your birth. This is not to say that the world is fair or just. It isn't, in spades. But now more than ever it is easier to do whatever you want without as much of the prejudice that held previous generations back. It is also easier to think that because no one is holding you back, if you are not successful in your terms at the path you have chosen, there is no one to blame but yourself.

So you are anxious. I think a lot about anxiety, as it happens, because I am the sort of anthropologist who looks at emotions, particularly the disturbing ones, which means that I immerse myself in a community and try to figure out what people feel, how they understand those feelings, and what they do about them. One of the things you learn fast in my line of work is that most people don't think of themselves as caught within a fine web of social structure. They think that they feel bad because they *are* bad, in some way, or at least that they are not very good at coping. In other words, you think you are anxious because you're afraid that you're not clever enough or tough enough to manage at the University of Chicago. I think you are anxious because of the social role you occupy at the dawn of the twenty-first century, because you have so much apparent freedom to choose and so many apparent opportunities that it can freeze you like a startled rabbit in the headlights of an oncoming car.

What earthly good can it do to read Weber, Marx, and Durkheim when you are trying to decide whether to be a neuroscientist or a science fiction writer, or when your earnest parents want you to be a doctor and you are trying to drum up the nerve to tell them you are planning a career in jazz ballet? A liberal arts education, if you use it wisely, teaches you how to make choices because it shows you how other people have chosen. Most people sit in the mud-puddle of their own fretful fears, peering out at the world through protective goggles. We all live in what the psychiatrist Jerome Frank called "assumptive worlds," sets of assumptions we make about the world that seem so natural, so commonsensical, that their very existence as assumptions fades until they become as real as concrete. I think about these assumptive worlds when I hold office hours. When I teach a class, everyone in the classroom has exactly the same data about me. They've all heard the same lectures and seen me wear the same clothes and make the same gestures. Yet when members of that class come to see me one by one, it turns out that they each have very different ideas about the sort of person I am and how they should treat me. The person who comes at three o'clock assumes that I'm a big sister and the person who comes at 3:15 expects me to be a judge, and for each of them, those assumptions are reasonable based on what they know of the world, based on the assumptions they have drawn from their own experience about the way the world proceeds. That's fine for office hours. It's not so fine for making life choices, because the world is more complex than you are able to perceive when looking out at it through muddy goggles from your puddle. And you can't just decide to abandon those assumptions about how the world works because to you they are not assumptions, but iron facts. You no longer realize that you invented them in the first place. As the old saying has it, fish can't tell you much about the water. They don't know it's there. But the courses you take here can give you the tools to clamber out of the puddle, or at least to see the water, if you treat the authors you read as people like yourselves, struggling to make sense of the world, desperately trying to figure out what kinds of moral and intellectual commitments are worth making, what kind of life is worth living. Nearly everyone you read in the core was once an anxious eighteen-year-old. He or she made a decision about what was worth writing about and why, and if you take as your task the burden of trying to understand deeply what the author thought was important to argue for and against and why, you will understand how his or her commitments were forged. And that will help you to understand and manage the forging of your own. At the heart of a liberal education stands the oldest human paradox: that the more deeply and intimately you understand other human beings—the more you understand their unique predicaments and their idiosyncratic pain—the more clearly you will see yourselves. If you would follow the inscription at Delphi—to know thyself—know others first.

In short, one aim of education is to improve your capacity for empathy. By that I do not mean a feel-good state of squishy oneness. I mean that if you genuinely try to understand—to read with compassion for the difficulty of the problem the writer was trying to solve and respect for the way he or she tried to solve it, to read from the inside out, trying to understand the author from the author's perspective, located in his or her time and space, struggling with the same existential issues that bother you but struggling with them in a way that is specific, historically particular, unique, you will be in a position to think. And thinking, as the anthropologist Clifford Geertz has pointed out, is a moral act. Anthropology is in the peculiar position of doing with real people what most scholars do with texts. When you read *The Grapes of Wrath,* you feel the suffocating dust of the baked, cracked ground and the despair of the migrant farmhands who traveled west on empty promises and a car strung together with twisted wire, but then you can close the book. When you do fieldwork with homeless women in a drop-in shelter, as I have done, you smell the clothes a woman cannot wash and you feel her terror of having nowhere to go that is safe, and then at the end of the interview the woman sometimes screams at you or hugs you and there is no way to pretend that you are detached and distant and purely scientific. You react with moral outrage—at the society, at the institution, sometimes at the women themselves—and then you have to hold back your judgment, and try to understand. This is what all great writing does, if we let it; it grabs at our guts and we respond to it, and then we have to step back, to understand. Geertz points out that the impossibility of separating your scholarly work from your life forces you to recognize that thinking well demands that we tolerate the enormous tension between our initial moral reaction and our scientific observation. Thinking is a moral act because it is a commitment to understand first and then to judge. And that tension is what forces us to grow and teaches us to choose and makes us who we become. Somewhere Picasso remarks that if you hope to draw a circle that is uniquely your own, you should try to draw a circle that is as true to geometric form as you can. You will fail to draw that perfect circle, but only in the attempt to thrust yourself away will you find the virtue of your own perspective.

This may seem like counterintuitive advice. Many young Americans think that to know themselves they need to find themselves, and they hold the naive belief that if they could just strip off everyday life like layers of an onion they would reach their true core, unadulterated by other people's expectations and the distractions of a fast-paced world. They believe that they have a true core, an essence, and that it sits inside of them waiting to be discovered, and that once they find it they will know whether they ought to be a doctor or a lawyer or a philosophy professor. Sometimes these young people go to Europe and work their way through Mediterranean countries picking grapes, confident that their true self will emerge somewhere en route to Italy. But people who believe that the self is like an onion and their true self is its core have not spent much time in the kitchen. Peel an onion down to its core and all you will find is air. You are not an untouched core. You are and will become the sum of your commitments, your choices—moral, intellectual, and practical—they amount to much the same thing in the end. To find yourself, don't dig under the surface of your life. Look at what you actually do, at what you come to care for, at what you fight to defend. Look at the small choices you make every day in the classroom, in the way that you read and interpret and argue, and the big choices will sort themselves out by themselves.

To help you on your way, I have a few pieces of Wise Advice. I should say that in contemplating this address, I thought perhaps I could bypass my own part in this and simply play the Baz Luhrmann sunscreen song, on the grounds that Baz and I must meet somewhere on the family tree. I'll content myself with reminding you that the song points out that

> [a]dvice is a form of nostalgia. Dispensing it is a way of fishing the past from the disposal, wiping it off, painting over the ugly parts and recycling it for more than it's worth.

For what it's worth, here is my advice:

RULE NO. 1

Never answer an important question in the abstract. It's just too easy to import all your assumptions and prejudices and never grasp what the question is really asking. Dormitory rooms were built for late-night discussions about whether God exists, for example, and the question of divine ontology is definitely worth debating. But do not delude yourself into thinking that your logical conclusions will actually tell you anything about how and when people reach towards spirituality. Several years ago, two of my oldest friends found themselves in trouble. Each had a young son diagnosed with a terrible illness. They had gone to the same schools and they came from similar backgrounds. They even married men of similar religious persuasions. One of them told me, as her son lay near death, that she could no longer accept even the possibility that there might be a god. No god, she said, could inflict this agony upon her toddler. The other friend told me that her son's death brought her closer to God, and for the same reason. The incomprehensible injustice, the irrationality, of her child's pain was beyond tolerating. Only God's love could help her bear it.

Whether or not God and the devil live in the details, people certainly do. Their lives are formed in the tiny fissures of the everyday, in the way they cuddle their dog and care for their car and in whether they eat cereal for breakfast. The anthropologist Claude Lévi-Strauss once wrote about what he called the science of the concrete. What he meant by this was that the so-called primitive mind was not dumb for lack of a physics or a higher mathematics. People who live in the neolithic world, for example, the forest-dwelling Amazonian Nambikwara, do not know only what they eat and use; they have an enormous curiosity about the forest, and they can identify hundreds of plants that the poor anthropologist cannot even distinguish. Among people like the Nambikwara, Lévi-Strauss said, "Animals and plants are not known as a result of their usefulness; they are deemed to be useful or interesting because they are first of all known" (*The*

Savage Mind, p. 9). And as they are known so are they ordered, so that from the little details in people's lives you can come to see the categories and principles they live by. Pay attention to the details of your life and of other lives, and learn from those details the driving passions of those lives. You will understand people more deeply; you will also, in the paradoxical mode I am advocating, come to see the world with utter uniqueness, your own. The great thinkers you will read in the core are first and foremost great observers who paid enormously careful attention to phenomena others had seen before but never noticed. A near fanatical attention to detail brought Darwin to evolution, Freud to the dynamic unconscious, and Marx to the labor theory of value. The world hasn't looked the same since. Find your own science of the concrete.

RULE NO. 2

Distrust pretension. I read an essay some time ago that much improved my enjoyment of certain types of academic discourse. You know E. B. White as the author of *Charlotte's Web* and *Stuart Little,* but you may not know that he was also perhaps the finest essayist America has produced and co-author of a lovely little book called *The Elements of Style.* In the conservative 1950s he wrote an essay that was ostensibly about politicians. White was an ardent Democrat and, in the spirit of his time, he felt that he should have sharp, clear views on political issues and on what Democrats were doing about them. The essay I like so much was written—again, ostensibly—about three Democrats whose writings White was trying to read one afternoon. He called them bedfellows because he was reading them when he was sick in bed. In the essay, White wrote about the way Truman distrusted the press for being too critical and the way Stevenson distrusted the public for not being critical enough. He pointed out that Acheson praised the loyalty and security measures Democrats first set in place in 1947 and that Acheson then went on to show how they undermined the freedoms they had initially set out to protect.

But the essay is really about Fred. Fred was a dachshund who died in 1948, before the essay was written, but for many years Fred had gallantly allowed White to take care of him. Fred was another one of White's bedfellows. In fact White wrote that he only took the Democrats to bed with

E. B. White and Fred at work for *The New Yorker* magazine

him for want of a dachshund and that he still missed Fred's smell, which was as evocative to his mind, he said, as a sudden whiff of cow barn. White wrote that although birds fascinated Fred,

> [h]is real hope as he watched the big shade trees outside the window was that a red squirrel would show up. When he sighted a squirrel, Fred would straighten up from his pillow, tense his frame, and then, in a moment or two, begin to tremble. The knuckles of his big forelegs, unstable from old age, would seem to go into spasm, and he would sit there with his eyes glued on the squirrel and his front legs alternately collapsing under him and bearing his weight again. ("Bedfellows," p. 102)

The reader of this essay which is ostensibly about politicians but really turns out to be about Fred only gradually understands that for White they have become the same topic. After a little more about Fred, White returned to the subject of politics and an argument, then as now a craggy hill in the political landscape, that prayer is a part of democracy. White didn't think that it was, but he also thought that democracy was a sort of faith, and he worried that in light of this his own views were a trifle inconsistent. And then he pauses, one feels, and draws breath. He remarks to the reader that these politicians are all such sober, thoughtful people. They work to improve and preserve and maintain in good repair this marvelous thing that is American society. Their earnestness, and their sense that this is possible, he implies, is a wonderful thing, and it helps him to feel confident in the face of creeping cynicism. They also remind him of Fred.

> It makes me eager to rise and meet the new day, as Fred used to rise to his, with the complete conviction that through vigilance and good work all porcupines, all cats, all skunks, all squirrels, all houseflies, all footballs, all evil birds in the sky could successfully be brought to account and the scene made safe and pleasant for the sensible individual—namely, him. (p. 198)

These days, when I read a sophisticated book full of high theory with words so abstract and metaphorical I feel I'd need to read a hundred more books to really get a grip, I no longer feel intimidated and vaguely inadequate. I simply settle into my chair, imagine the author as an eighteen-inch dachshund, and ask myself, So what's his squirrel?

RULE NO. 3

Buy Strunk and White's *The Elements of Style.* The book is an advocate of clear and precise language. At one point, they take a fine moment in the English language and recast it in lugubrious modern prose. Actually, what they do is to borrow the recasting from George Orwell, a kindred spirit and another fine essayist similarly aggrieved at the contemporary mangling of the English tongue. Here is the original, from the King James translation of Ecclesiastes:

> I returned, and saw under the sun, that the race is not to the swift, nor the battle to the strong, neither yet bread to the wise, nor yet riches to men of understanding, nor yet favor to men of skill; but time and chance happeneth to them all.

Here is Orwell, in modern English:

> Objective consideration of contemporary phenomena compels the conclusion that success or failure in competitive activities exhibits no tendency to be commensurate with innate capacity, but that a considerable element of the unpredictable must inevitably be taken into account.

Read this little book before you write any essays yourself. If you want to give your professors a hard time, read it again when you read anything they have written.

RULE NO. 4

Find a writing partner. Just as it is hard to look at your own assumptions and see them as they are, it is hard to read Strunk and White and see your own crabbed sentences for what they actually say, free of the shimmering prose you wrote in your own imagination. It's much easier to pick out the pompous phrase and passive voice in someone else's paper. Choose someone you think you trust among your classmates and edit each other's papers. You don't need to be in the same classes together. You don't even need to know anything about each other's subjects. Exchange your papers, and mark the spots in your partner's paper where you got bored or restless or confused, and then look at the places your partner has marked on yours. Refrain from explaining to such loyal friends their many weaknesses as readers of your prose. Just try to figure out what made your best intentions misleading or unclear to someone who was actually trying to help. If you can do that—and it's not easy—you will write papers that get better every time. If you can learn to write, you can learn to write well, and if you can write well, you can command your destiny.

RULE NO. 5

Know that as you change, the way you understand will also change. Have compassion for the person you are right now. The novelist Mary Gordon wrote that she read George Eliot's *Middlemarch* three times. When she was sixteen, she read it for its breathless romance, and she yearned for Eliot's heroine Dorothea to marry the dashing young Will Ladislaw. The first summer after college, she read it again and found herself suffused with feminist outrage at Eliot, who assumed that Dorothea should live out her life on other people's terms, defined by the men she married. When Gordon was in her forties, she read *Middlemarch* yet again, and this time she understood for the first time that it was a sad book, because it saw so clearly the way all lives are carved out by character and circumstance, how so often the gifts we have are left unused or undeveloped because of events we could not have foreseen and choices we could not allow ourselves to make. Ask of yourself as much as you possibly can, but recognize that your achievements and your failures alike will be in part the result of simple luck. Enjoy the way you will change and embrace your widening understanding. Look back on the person you have been with respect for all you accomplished despite the rain.

| RULE NO. 6, MY LAST

Laugh. Back around the time of the Second World War, when social sciences were thought to be invincible and foundations gave grants to sociologists, economists, and anthropologists with the idea that with a little research they would figure out how to win the war on poverty and then go out and do it, a group of social scientists at Harvard University decided to figure out what made people successful. As an aside, foundations still give grants to people who hope to end poverty, but these days everyone seems more humble, both about whether the solution will be a good one and about whether anyone will pay attention even if it is. Democracy, as Plato pointed out, is a mixed blessing. So is science. Once, for reasons too complicated to explain, I found myself talking to a nuclear weapons scientist at Lawrence Livermore National Laboratory who was demoralized and distressed about the way, he said, that nuclear weapons science had gotten out of hand in general and into the wrong hands in particular. At one point he interrupted his diatribe and looked at me and said, "You social scientists have thought a lot about society. You should just take over the government and tell people who to marry and where to live and what to do." It was a fine, but rare, moment.

In any event, back around the time of the Second World War, some people at Harvard decided that they should select the best and brightest undergraduates and follow them for the course of their lives. They interviewed them and had them evaluated by an array of doctors, nurses, psychologists, vocational counselors, and psychiatrists. They weighed them and surveyed them and made them fill out innumerable charts and tests. They presented them with a series of ambiguous pictures and asked them for the story each picture brought to their minds. They sat down with their mothers and collected childhood anecdotes. They even recorded their brain waves. After the young men graduated—they were, of course, all young men and for that matter white, middle class, and northeastern seaboard men—they followed them with long questionnaires and more surveys and charts and interviews. They kept track of how much they earned and how often they missed work and whether they got divorced and how many kids they had. They sent questionnaires to their wives. More than twenty-five years later, when the study subjects were forty-seven, a young psychiatrist, George Vaillant, was hired to make sense of the data. He chose one hundred of the men to interview yet again and went around the country to meet them one by one.

Not surprisingly, some men had done better than others on conventional measures of success. These conventional measures reflected the era of the study and included whether the man earned more than his father; whether he liked his job; and whether he had been promoted steadily. They included whether he had maintained a marriage for at least ten years and whether he would describe his present marriage as "good"; whether he had children and whether those children were doing well or markedly underperforming; whether he had many friends; whether he enjoyed good physical health; and whether he took vacations (just in case you wondered, taking vacations was regarded as a sign of mental health).

One knew that there would be people who did well on the conventional measures. What was more surprising was that this success was associated with a particular psychological pattern, what Vaillant called "a mature defensive style." Human life is not easy. Bad things happen to good people, often at the worst possible time. The men in this study with the best life outcomes, Vaillant said, were not men who had avoided pain, but men who handled great unhappiness with humor, with sublimation, with altruism, and with anticipation. These are called defenses because when bad things happen, we try to defend ourselves from the onslaught on our psyches. Some bad things are sudden and unexpected and big. You will get a phone call. Someone you love has died. Other bad things are slow and subtle, and some are almost embarrassingly small. Your parents have a distant, failing marriage. You do badly on an exam. The girl you ask out says no. There are many different ways to respond to the insults the world throws out at you. You can deny that it ever happened so it doesn't bother you. Some people actually forget, for a little while at least, that they ever answered the phone. You can decide that the person who caused the pain is evil, so it doesn't really matter. You can pretend it doesn't hurt. You can know it hurts and get in a car and drive really, really fast, as if you could leave it behind forever. You can be angry at your professor but blow up at your roommate instead. All of us have employed every one of these defensive habits at different moments. Vaillant used all his surveys and graphs and interviews to argue that the men who reached the age of forty-seven with the most successful careers, the most satisfying marriages, and the best physical health in his study had been more likely to respond to the world's curve balls with grace, laughing at what they could and channeling their disappointment into productivity. Mental health, he said, is not about the absence of unhappiness, but about the way you manage it.

Vaillant knew that his study had limitations. The conventional criteria did not account for the creative artist at all, and he was uneasy about how well they would judge women and how American and middle class and mid-century they were. Still, there is some wisdom in the study. College life can be difficult, and you are anxious. If you can learn to soothe your anxiety by worrying more about Durkheim's problems than about your own, if you can laugh at the absurdity of the grading system and still work to make your papers more convincing, if you conquer your shyness by learning to dance, your year will be more enjoyable and the journey of discovery more exciting. You have already made more choices than you realize. One of the better ones was choosing the University of Chicago. Welcome to the Class of 2007. ○

TANYA LUHRMANN delivered this address on September 25, 2003, when she was Professor in the Committee on Human Development, the Committee on Human Culture, and the College. She is now Professor of Anthropology and Psychology at Stanford University.

robert pippin

liberation and the liberal arts

2000

It is a great privilege to be invited to give this annual talk to the incoming class. The "Aims of Education" speech has become a ritual at the University of Chicago for the last thirty-eight years, and I am honored to be able to deliver the address to the first class of the new millennium, and in the presence of our new president, Don Randel, whom I welcome most enthusiastically and gratefully to this truly ungovernable place. However much a great honor, though, it is also very intimidating. It is intimidating not only because, with a topic so sweeping and complicated, avoiding clichés is hard, but for another, obvious reason. This choice of yours about where to go to college is one of the three or four "big ones" in your life, right up there with the choice of a career and a spouse. You all no doubt took advice from parents and relatives and friends, and probably, for some of you, your decision was affected as much by where you weren't accepted as by where you were. But all of you decided to apply *here*, and the decision to come here was, for many of you, the first major life decision that you yourselves, as adults determining your own fate, have made. It will shape so much in your future that many of you are no doubt starting to think: well, why *did* I come here? This place seems so intense and serious; what in the world *have* I gotten myself into? And you might be expecting me to tell you, and that is what is so intimidating.

After all, yours is a unique and extremely privileged situation, and that always calls for reflection of some sort. Only an infinitesimally small percentage of people in the world your age get four years like this, and only a minority of those privileged few, I am sorry to have to say, really take advantage of such an opportunity. Unless we can start a conversation about what this unique structure and rare opportunity is all for, and can settle together on some common aspirations, we might as well drop the pretense of great seriousness that events like this are supposed to imply, import the fraternities and sororities from Florida State and USC, build the engineering schools, drop the Common Core, and "vocationalize" away. As already noted, this is the period of your lives when *you* start to take over the active management of your own affairs, when you begin to "lead" those lives, as we say, and in North America (almost alone in the world, apart from the Oxbridge system in England), we have settled on the residential liberal arts college as an ideal way to help you do so, to make part of this transition. Why is that?

| TWO

Let me start with the truisms often uttered in contexts like this. Truisms are, after all, occasionally *true*, and they can thus be a good beginning guide. The chief aim of education at the University of Chicago is a successful "liberal arts" education. (To avoid the confusing suggestion that you might be here to learn only painting and music and dance, the "arts" bit is now often dropped and this phrase is shortened to a "liberal education." But that can be confusing too, since it suggests that you are here to learn to be more like Ted Kennedy or

Mario Cuomo. So I might as well stick with the old fashioned term, according to which biology and economics, just as much as literature and philosophy can be studied as a liberal art if studied in a certain way.) Perhaps no other university in the country takes such an ideal so seriously or asks itself so interminably what exactly a liberal arts education is, and whether it is so all-fired important. The topic usually arises here in discussions about general education and the Core. (This is the place after all that once had a four year, common core requirement!) But it also describes an ideal to which we all aspire throughout the student's time here and that general ideal already evinces the root meaning in the ideal of a "liberality of mind"; that is, the realization of a certain sort of *freedom*. The Latin root, *liber*, means "free" (it is also the Latin noun for "book," an odd coincidence that supports the point I am trying to make), and the very first use of the word "liberal" in English in 1375 was as an adjective in "the liberal arts" and designated "*the objects of study worthy of a free person.*" And that is what we are supposed to teach you: to enable you to become a freer person and this by showing you (so goes that truism) how to "think for yourself," to be able to reflect critically on what you have heretofore just taken for granted; and to learn to do this by an acquaintance with the best that has been thought and written by human beings. Similarly, as you all have also probably heard, here you should not just learn the facts and methodologies of modern mathematics and science; you should learn how a mathematician and a scientist thinks, so that you too can go forth and design your own experiments and proofs (or appreciate that form of discovery and reasoning when you encounter it "in the real world"), just as you can learn to think your own thoughts and write your own elegant, persuasive English prose.

In a university setting such a liberality of mind means attention to "knowledge for its own sake" and so a certain kind of freedom *from* the compulsion of the requirements of biological life, from the satisfaction of unavoidable needs, the press of the passions, the everyday and the practically necessary. (This understanding of freedom, which is obviously connected with a kind of leisure and privilege, was first formulated and defended over 2,000 years ago by Aristotle and has influenced the notion of an "ideal" education ever since.) You all know the caricature of such an "impractical" attitude: the absent minded professor, who is *so* indifferent to the practical that he forgets to change clothes and to eat and so forth. That is a figure of ridicule of course, but it is also, oddly, an expression of envy and in its latent hostility a kind of suspicion that such a type really can exist with such indifference to the practical world; that he or she really *is* so liberated from such cares and can lead a life dedicated to something believed to be of intrinsic value. The opposite of the liberal arts stance or sensibility is then not just dogmatism and prejudice, but also any kind of over-specialized technical instruction, or vocationalism, a slavish devotion to the means necessary for mere surviving or existing comfortably, rather than a devotion to inquiry about the good or the best life, and to the value of knowledge itself, for its own sake. Or at least that was the older controversy when our most famous former president, Robert Maynard Hutchins, strode through these hallowed halls; and it is a debate that is still very relevant.

More recently the suspicion about such a claim to freedom has come from the charge that the traditional humanistic liberal arts ideal that comes down to us from the Renaissance, the general ideal that I have just summarized, is itself not liberating but in the service of some political goal, and rather than foster liberation, actually "serves power" in some way (a class, a gender, an imperial power), reproduces an enslavement to an elite or to a restrictive, exclusionary self-understanding. But this last charge is of course not really an objection to the liberal arts ideal, but an attempt to formulate and pursue it more rigorously, even more "purely."

THREE

As this simple summary already indicates, any formulation of such a liberal arts ideal (the view that a certain sort of learning and knowledge might enable one to lead a freer life, even if a learning and knowledge not directly connected with practical results or technical power) is an ideal often formulated in response to and as a defense against a perceived threat or attack (such as that pursuit of such an ideal is a waste of time). The very beginning of this series of lectures at the University of Chicago was understood as a "response" to such a "threat" when the then Dean of the College, Alan Simpson, wrote to the Ford Foundation in 1961 requesting funds for a lecture series on the aims of education because, he claimed, the ideal of a liberal education was "under pressure everywhere." Many of the talks presented in this series have that same tone, responding to various intellectual, economic, professional and practical "attacks" on the attempt to achieve this liberality of mind through reading books and learning science.

There are lots and lots of reasons for this frequent siege mentality and "man the barricades" rhetoric. For one things, suspicion of the humanistic university ideal might go *very* deep in the modern world we live in. The university after all, is like the Roman Catholic Church or the military.

Together with these, it was one of the very, very few pre-modern or feudal institutions to make it through the wrenching process of European modernization and to survive in some recognizable form into the modern world. (For all such institutions, even the funny, medieval way that we sometimes dress, with robes and gowns and medals and sashes, somehow survived; not to mention all this gothic architecture.) But even though universities survived, the tone of suspicion and anxiety about such old institutions in a much altered modern world can be felt everywhere when the very words "scholastic" or "academic" or "ivory tower" and so forth are mentioned as obvious disparagements. And so here we will all sit one day soon, with bio-technology professors on the "cutting," even Frankensteinean edge of modern research, dressed at graduation in the same thirteenth century robes as the Latin Professor and theologian. It's an odd place indeed.

That problem of a "fit" in modernity is even worse in the humanities and interpretive social sciences, where an internal crisis of legitimacy has been going on for a couple of hundred years now. Such disciplines of course, like philosophy and literature and history, purport to know something about human beings and the human world that is worth knowing. Because of this we even insist here that you can't get a degree without grappling for a while with what they claim. But everybody also knows that the seats of power and influence in the modern university are the natural and life sciences. (The exception is economics, but its prestige is largely a result of its mathematical complexity—it certainly doesn't stem from its predictive power—and its ever growing "market share" of undergraduate audiences.) The sciences have an accepted method for resolving debate and moving on; what they know *works*, and they have given human beings a kind of power not even imagined in ancient mythologies. Prior to World War II, the tone and aura of medieval universities could still be felt at the elite institutions. University presidents were often classicists (perhaps musicologists); English and history were often the most popular majors; studying science was a bit plebeian, common, even, I was once told, "smelly." After the war, and especially after the cold war and sputnik and the cost of Big Science and the war on cancer and the breakthroughs of molecular biology and now neurology, everything has changed. And it would be odd indeed if the "liberal arts ideal" did not look and feel different to new generations of students and educators. So besides these general considerations about the status of the liberal arts ideal in modern history, perhaps the first thing we need to talk about is the relation between this ideal and the various specific pressures that have come to challenge, even threaten it, and especially those historical pressures that have emerged in the last fifty years or so. We often understand this ideal best, in other words, in terms of what opposes it, offers itself as an alternative, and there is a lot more to say about this history. What I'd like to do then, after a brief survey of the recent history of American universities, is to talk then a little bit about the ideal itself in that context, and so to return to this question of the free, or at least the freer life that we have promised you.

FOUR

We need first to understand what a different sort of place this is, in the context of contemporary "post-secondary" or "higher" education. There are now 12.3 million undergraduate students in such post-secondary schools. (I heard a fine talk a year and a half ago about this subject by a literature professor at the City University of New York, Louis Menand, and I refer here to some of the statistics that he compiled. The figures are now a bit out of date, but the corresponding percentages have stayed the same.) Almost half of these attend two year community colleges, some 5.5 million. So there are 6.8 million of you in bachelor degree programs. The vast majority of these, some 4.6 million, are enrolled in public colleges and universities. So that leaves about 2 million of you (out of this 12.3 million) enrolled in private, non-profit, four-year colleges. But there are all sorts of such colleges, ranging from Bob Jones University to Bennington, and if we look at the truly exclusive, very hard to get into, very expensive liberal arts colleges (that is, those that charge over $20,000 tuition), there are only about 100,000 students, or less than 1 percent of students now in college or university.

Now Chicago is hard to characterize in this group. Like a very few other top universities, we have taken the liberal arts college idea from medieval British universities like Oxford and Cambridge, and combined it with the idea of the research university, pioneered in Germany in the early nineteenth century. And again, we are not talking about very many such universities; the Ivy League, Chicago, Stanford, Duke, Johns Hopkins, Rochester, Washington University and a couple more. But even if we look at *all* the major research universities, including the majority which do not have a liberal arts college, only about half of the students who go *there* major in a liberal art and get a bachelor's degree in such a humanities or in a pure, research oriented social or natural science. Twenty percent of all B.A.s in the U.S. are now awarded in business; 10 percent in education;

7 percent in the health professions. When I taught at the University of California, by far the biggest undergraduate major, and growing every year, was "communications," whatever that is. It has been reported that there are almost twice as many undergraduate degrees conferred every year in a field that calls itself "protective services" as in all foreign languages and literatures combined.

So the category of "higher education" is a *huge* tent, with all kinds of various beasts in it, so much so that there may be no such thing as "*the* American higher education system." Moreover, if we also look historically just at the study of the liberal arts, apart from the institutional question, then we can note another motive for the siege mentality. The proportion of undergraduate degrees awarded annually in the liberal arts has been declining for a hundred years now (apart from a brief increase between 1955 and 1970). And this slide is all greatly complicated by one development: the fact that we are now living, or have been living since around 1975 or so, in a period of a massive, unstable, nervous reaction to the greatest expansionary period in the history of education anywhere. Between 1945 and 1975 the number of American undergraduates increased by almost 500 percent and the number of graduate students (and this is truly an amazing figure) increased by nearly *900 percent*. More professors were hired in the 1960s alone than had been hired in the 325-year history of American higher education to that point.

What happened then, after and in reaction to this great expansion, is complicated, but it is at least obvious that in this super-heated period, colleges and universities had over-expanded and a period of retrenchment and cut-back was in order. The draft and the Vietnam war ended; so did the baby-boomer surge in the demographics, and a very serious recession, mysteriously accompanied by runaway inflation, set in. Universities and colleges, facing rapidly declining applications and declining admissions had to compete ferociously for students, and students themselves faced post-college prospects far more uncertain and competitive than at any time in the history of the Republic. Said in a simple formula, the liberal arts—study, reflection and learning for its own liberating sake—require a certain sort of leisure, security, and peace. In a situation of anxiety, uncertainty and competition, such a climate can be ever rarer. Obviously all these pressures since 1975 have changed the atmosphere of higher education, bringing with it some healthy forms of skepticism and doubt about some of the old liberal art verities, but also a great uncertainty and anxiety among, and a great pressure on, the liberal arts faculty. This sometimes led to a furious and near suicidal self-criticism, or an attempt at a kind of populism, a populist attack on the high culture/low culture distinction, or an odd, dizzying, nervous susceptibility to academic fads (or market trends), new ones year in and year out. (And actually the effects of such anxiety and uncertainty about exactly what "college is for" can be charted even before 1975. In the period between 1962 and 1983, the percentage of students who majored in foreign languages and literatures declined by 58 percent; in philosophy they declined by 60 percent; in English by 72 percent, and in mathematics by 67 percent. Where did they all go? Well, in that same period, the number of business majors increased 87 percent.) So while intuitively, one might think that a place like the University of Chicago has the resources and the reputation and clout and faculty to think of itself as simply doing better what all universities aspire to do; that we represent a kind of peak, the Platonic Ideal or perfection of what universities should be and what other places cannot afford to be, in a situation like this, where we look so different from what goes on in the rest of the 99 percent of post-secondary education, it is not hard to imagine why this system might feel under threat, and why they and we might feel that we have become an anachronism; hardly a perfection.

In other words, over-expansion, market uncertainties, economic anxiety, the need to justify the expense of a college education in terms of a good rate of return in future employment have all made that 99 percent to 1 percent ratio even more significant, has increased the pressure on places like Chicago to move to the norm, and can make the ideal of a certain sort of freedom from practical concerns seem so unrealistic, when the jockeying for position in the practical world is so intense. The idea, in this climate, of concentrating on Elizabethan literature or linguistics or astrophysics or Greek philosophy can look a little like playing solitaire on the deck of a sinking Titanic. (And, by the way, we are about to look even more different in the years ahead. The experts say that the next waves in higher education will be for-profit universities and on-line or distance learning—very likely some combination of both of these—and if those catch on and start to dominate the market then *residential* liberal arts colleges with merit-based, need-blind admissions and some sort of education in a core curriculum, might begin to look to the general public like fox hunting clubs or monasteries.)

FIVE

So that was (by and large anyway) the original hope for the liberal arts, and those are the pressures that seem to be squeezing it. In the face of that pressure, what can be said for the liberal arts ideal?

In terms of the practical survival of that ideal and such colleges, the right response is probably, "Who knows?" My guess is that there is no great danger that Chicago will be turning out sanitation engineers, disc jockeys and industrial arts majors anytime soon. There will always be people who find a home in books and research, and always be those who are smart enough to know that there is much of intrinsic value for the rest of their lives in wrestling for a while with difficult ideas and in appreciating the beauty of mathematics or science. Remember that we probably need, all of us in this small boat, only a couple of hundred thousand recruits a year or so, and it's a big country. The ultimate fate of the *ideal*, the strength of belief in it, commitment to it, its perseverance over the next century or two centuries, is another matter. That depends on what we believe about it and how we believe it. I would like to spend the second half of this talk discussing that.

SIX

Imagine that the question is whether you are here at the University of Chicago *freely*, *of your own free will*; whether your coming here reflects or expresses you, whether you can see yourself in this kind of role. Obviously the first condition that has to be satisfied for you to be able to answer "yes" is that no one coerced or forced or tricked you into coming here. If your parents told you that you had gotten into Brown, drove you here and dropped you off, you would have a clear case that *you* did not come here freely; this was not your doing. Likewise with being coerced or threatened to come here, and I certainly hope none of you has any such stories to tell.

These are all fairly obvious, external conditions. No one or nothing from "the outside" should be constraining or coercing or unduly pushing or pulling. But there are also clearly "internal" conditions that have to be satisfied. You have to be able to stand in the right relation to your own life for your being here to be the result of a free choice. No one may have coerced or forced or tricked you to be here, but, for example, if you have felt absolutely obsessed since your were six years old with the idea of going to the University of Chicago, and have no idea why, then you also did not come here freely, even though nobody else, just you, is responsible for your coming here. Compulsions like this are rare and the example is fanciful of course, but the possibility already illuminates one of the oldest ideas about freedom in the Western tradition. This is that the only real form of genuine unfreedom or true slavery is ignorance; the only true form of freedom is wisdom, ultimately knowledge of what is best. In this fanciful case, unless you have some idea of why it is better for you to be here rather than anywhere else or at any other university or whatever, then you did not *come here freely*. There is an element of alienation or strangeness *to you* in your presence here. Some crucial part of your life, while it was in fact produced *by you*, does not truly reflect the "you" that you understand yourself to be and identify with, and so this decision cannot in the deepest sense *be* yours.

And this sort of intuition represents something essential to the notion of liberation, liberality of mind, or freedom, promised by a liberal arts education. Now this idea, some of you may have begun to wonder, already may sound a bit suspect. ("Is this guy telling us that the main reason to come here is to be able to find out later why we really came here and whether it was really a good idea?") Well, yes, that is what I am trying to say, and I hope it does not sound as strange as that formulation makes it. There are a very great many elements, terms, values, aspirations, that have gone into the decisions you have made and will make that are so opaque and mysterious to you, to all of us, that we cannot really be said to be masters of decisions that rely on them.

| SEVEN

Think of it this way. in one of his many hilarious novels about modern campus life, the British novelist David Lodge depicts a game played by particularly brave (and quite drunk) professors. The point of this game is to admit something even more embarrassing than the professor who went before you, to try to trump your predecessor and ultimately to trump everyone else by revealing the most truly embarrassing, humiliating fact about yourself. What each of them is trying to do is to name a book that, given his or her academic specialty, it would be taken for granted that he or she had read several times, but which they had in fact never read. So if a professor of Elizabethan literature admits that he has never read *Hamlet*, the next person, say a philosophy professor must try to top that, by admitting say, that she had never read anything by Plato. And then the German professor would have to admit that he couldn't read anything by Thomas Mann because the German was too difficult, and then the history professor would have to admit that even though he was a leading expert in modern German history, he couldn't read German books at all. And so on.

It is not too difficult to imagine all of us playing a version of the game where we try to name an idea crucial to our understanding of ourselves and of the modern world, and which has played a critical role in some of our decisions, some of the policies we have formulated, and many of the judgments and even condemnations we have formulated about others, but which we have no clue how to define and, no matter how much we have relied on it, no clue at all how to defend the idea from objections. Examples come easily to mind to all of us. What, after all, is a "right"? What does the notion of a natural or human right mean to delineate? What *other* kinds are there? Why are we said to have them? How many do we have? Do we have a right to interesting jobs? To a cool pair of shoes? To own and eat animals? Why or why not? What do we mean when we say something is beautiful? If we claim that that term "means something different to each person" *what* is it that means something different to each person? How important is the beautiful? More important than the creation of more jobs? How much more or less important? Why do groups of strangers like to gather together in the dark and watch a small group of other people pretend to be people who they are not, doing absolutely horrible things to each other, while also pretending that they are not observed? Why do *you* do this, or what is the point of theater? When did we start to do this in our civilization, and what might explain this origin? Why did people just like us, perhaps in some sense, better than us, like George Washington and Thomas Jefferson, own slaves? Could you explain what a nuclear reaction really is? What it really means to be genetically disposed to something? And so on. The point of the game would be to admit something even more obviously important to you and some decision or judgment of yours than your predecessor's example, and which you would in principle have to defend in order to explain some action or opinion of yours, but which you could not claim to understand.

Being *better* able to do all that explaining and defending is clearly a kind of liberation because the more of such understanding you possess the more you are able to stand behind what you do, acknowledge it as your own, especially when challenged by others, *because* you can stand behind it, explain it and defend it to some degree, to yourself and others. Of course, there are writers and thinkers who believe that this is all a mistaken way to look at it. They believe that what you do more genuinely expresses you and is freely done only if we get rid of all this reflection and self-consciousness and opinions and theories which are very likely just views of others to which we have become subject, and that we should strive to achieve a state of ever more intense emotional immediacy, or spontaneity and direct expression, not filtered through theories and thoughts.

Well, pursuing these issues could take us pretty far afield. My version of the David Lodge game was only meant to illuminate in a very broad way why a better form of self-understanding might make it possible to say that you led a life more "your own." Around the sixteenth and seventeenth century or so, when it began to seem to many people that a life belonged essentially to the finite individual him- (and eventually her-) self, not to God, or to one's master or lord or fatherland or husband or father, the question of *how* we could come to acknowledge our deeds as truly *our* own, and the roles of self-consciousness and expanded knowledge in that possibility, loomed as large items on the agenda, and we are here, in the kind of university we have, partly because of all that.

| EIGHT

But I want to close with a final consideration about the role of books, research science, history, art, music—the academic enterprise—in this liberationist ideal. One way of understanding the possibility of a free life—"your own life"—is to consider which of your past decisions you could truly be said to be able to "stand behind," where that means being able to defend or justify them when challenged, or even which you could claim to understand. "Having reasons" in this sense for what you did, having something to say about "why," is a general condition for some event being considered an action of yours at all, and not having any reasons means it is very hard to understand *any* link between you and what conduct you engage in. If the question is why you came to the University of Chicago, or are concentrating in chemistry, or why you stopped speaking to a friend, and you replied, "I don't know, I just felt like it," it is very hard to see concentrating in chemistry or not speaking to a friend as any sort of deed performed *by* you. It really does look like something that happened to you rather than like something you did.

But if this is true, what is it to have such reasons, and *when* are they satisfying enough for the deeds to count as "claimed" by you, as yours? The issues that I have just been talking about assume that a *deeper* awareness of the possible options, a *broader* sense of the sorts of relevant justifications, a *better* familiarity with the most crucial possible positions and objections, and so forth, can be understood as "liberating," making such evaluations freer by in essence increasing *the quality of the reasons* you can give. The same can be said for understanding historical change and coming to understand why options are framed for us now as they are, why things used to seem so different, and for understanding other great civilizations and their histories. Such reasons become forms of thought that you do not just inherit, but can take up knowingly as your own. If this transition happens at all, it has to happen some time, and *this* is the time set aside for it to happen for a small group of young people; i.e., you and your colleagues in liberal arts colleges. If all this works well, where once one might have seen before one only a small, narrow path of decision with very few options, might look broader and more various, surrounded by less darkness and uncertainty; much that seemed necessary and fated, we could now understand, could have been otherwise, and might be otherwise in the future, and that is all certainly "liberating."

But it might also seem a bit unrealistic, even utopian. And so it would, if we think of all this as occurring simply because certain books are assigned in general education courses and certain courses are required. If a university prides itself simply on having assigned such books, and prides itself on insisting that students have a look at them, then most of what I have been saying would indeed be very hard to connect with such a self-satisfied and superficial notion of a "liberal arts education." It matters of course which books or themes make up a university's idea of itself, how much and what sort of math and science the university requires of its students. But what matters much more is the way in which faculty and students engage those books, or other books, or various ideas. And that essentially means the way they engage each other. Let me close with a remark about that.

NINE

Since almost everything of importance and controversy in human life involves some sort of normative question, a choice that demands evaluation and a decision about what ought to be or ought to be done, the issue of what sorts of reasons are appropriate, what it would be to be confidently in charge of one's existence is a vast, unmanageable topic here. But there is something peculiar about the nature of these reasons worth mentioning in a discussion about the liberal arts.

These evaluative questions, and the arguments about them, have special characteristics. On the one hand, the issues that are raised are unavoidable and as serious and important as one can imagine. On the other hand, there has hardly been the kind of convergence in our civilization about such evaluative issues that there has been about matters of fact. Most of you are intelligent enough to begin finding things to disagree with already in what I've said today. There is no decision procedure for any of this. In any such attempt to improve the quality of the reasons we give each other or are willing to accept, there is no equivalent to the test tube changing color if we get the right answer or the bacteria dying if we find the right drug. Our odds on being better warned against false leads, dead ends and so forth go up if we can find a way of learning from what the best minds ever had to say about all of this. But of course, the question of what Aristotle or Dante or Karl Marx really *meant* is just as disputed as any possible "answer" to such questions.

What then can we rely on for guidance in the pursuit of such issues; how could we hope for any sort of even small progress in such endeavors?

Well, the answer embodied in these liberal arts colleges is very simple. We depend on each other. After all, what it is to have a reason for what you believe, to be able to acknowledge it as yours, is to have something to offer to someone whom your action affects or injures or provokes to question you. And part of what it is for the reason to be adequate is for that offering to be accepted, at least ideally, in conditions where it is the proposed reason itself that is doing the persuading. Of course in deciding whether to accept what someone proposes, we are always looking to what, independent of us, might make the reason a good one, but that too is often in dispute, and the conversation then goes another round.

Put another way: I expect you'll discover shortly that a great deal of what goes on here is arguing; sometimes friendly, sometimes heated, and it can sometimes look like egotism, grandstanding, envy, or just plain bullying. But at bottom, this endless conversation we have invited you to join is a kind of "liberal arts research." We are always trying to find out what sort of reason will pass muster, among colleagues in the profession and here on campus, among professors and graduate students and among graduate students, and certainly and most frequently between professors and you, and among yourselves. By means of these conversations, we are both trying to hold each other in check, and to help each other see what sort of account or justification or interpretation might be adequate, might be enough. For this to work at all, we have to be able to hear you out; hence the emphasis on discussion seminars; you have to get to know each other relatively well; hence the idea of residential campuses; and we all have to approach this with the right attitude and openness; hence talks like this one. Someone out to convert people, to enlighten the ignorant, or even someone a little too quick and eager to think of himself as a radical critic, as "speaking truth to power" distort and impede this conversation. With the kinds of questions, of the magnitude and seriousness, that we all will discuss here, we have to depend pretty heavily on each other for any clarity and even partial satisfaction in addressing them, and none of that will work if you play the part of the timid, or the too-cool, or the angry, alienated student, and I play the part of the know it all, or the bored, aloof, arrogant professor, or the stand-up comic or ironic cynic. You will find, I think, that most of us will do our part, and it remains true every year that the University's traditions and the wise judgments of our admissions office ensure that it is very likely that most of you will too. Better conversations about great things make for better reasons, and better reasons make for freer lives. And as one of my favorite writers, Henry James, put it simply: 'Without your life, what have you got?"

You only get one college experience in your life, and my colleagues and I are not so modest that we can't say: we think that you have all chosen wisely in coming here. I urge you to enter this conversation rather than just listen to it, and, I hope I've made clear, I urge that not just for your sake, but for mine. Thank you for your attention on this warm afternoon, and, once again this week, welcome to the University of Chicago. ❍

ROBERT PIPPIN, the Evelyn Stefansson Nef Distinguished Service Professor in the John U. Nef Committee on Social Thought, the Department of Philosophy, and the College, delivered this address on September 19, 2000.

kenneth w. warren

education at odds

2007

It is an honor, and it is also very daunting, to stand before you today to speak about the aims of education here at the University of Chicago. Having in preparation for this talk taken the time to read previous addresses by my colleagues, I can tell you that everyone before me has felt equally honored and most have felt likewise daunted or intimidated, which means that up to this point I've told you nothing new. Also like me, many of my predecessors have desired not only your attention but also a cash advance on your sympathy so that if you happen to get bored or bothered by what we have to say you'll be more likely to say in turn, "Well it was a very difficult thing to do, so we shouldn't be too hard on the poor speaker."

Nonetheless you may be wondering about the "daunting" and "intimidating" part of this—that is, aside from the size of the audience gathered here, why shouldn't I find this a bit easy? After all, everyone who has delivered this address has been someone who has spent her or his entire adult life involved in higher education in one way or another, so it would seem reasonable to expect an "Aims" speaker to be quite comfortable in this role if it's just an exercise in describing what it is we do. But that's not quite right, is it? Describing what you're doing is not quite the same as describing what you are aiming at by doing it, particularly if by getting involved in higher education you might also be subjecting yourself to aims other than your own. So even if I were to redefine my task as something more manageable, say, speaking to you on the Aims of Teaching Literature, or the Aims of Teaching American Literature, or even the Aims of Teaching African American Literature, I would still fall short of the mark demanded here. To elaborate a bit, one way of describing what I do is to say that I try to make students like you feel that, for the time being, the most important task facing you in this world is, say, trying to figure out how to interpret the final paragraph of Henry James's novel, *The American.* I would stress the importance of this task, not because it would help you get a better grade in my course (which, of course it would), not because it would somehow make you a better person (which it might, although I wouldn't bet on it), and not because it would give you skills that you could apply to other tasks (although assuredly if you can read Henry James you do have some skills that will stand you in good stead elsewhere). No, my aim would be to have you devote yourself to producing the best understanding or best interpretation of that novel that you could—no more, no less.

But is that, I hope you are asking, aiming high enough? If that's all I'm up to then, on this view, higher education might be best represented not as an assembly or a synod in which august professors deliberate on the most effective way to organize a curriculum for higher purposes, but rather as something closer to a summer art fair in which each professor stands within a booth displaying and extolling his/her wares, not caring particularly what's being displayed in the surrounding booths so long as a steady stream of customers flows his or her way. It would be, then, only when the stream slowed to a trickle or threatened to dry up altogether that you might be forced to take a look around to see what was going on and discover that, say, huge crowds had gathered over at the booth marked "Economics" while only a stray customer managed to find her way into the booth marked "Classics." And if you happened to find yourself in the sparsely populated regions of this educational bazaar, you could respond in one of several ways: You could decide that this is indeed a marketplace of ideas and that those undertakings that fail to find paying customers, so to speak, should rightly give way to those enterprises that were drawing crowds. Or, you could steal a page from the other team's playbook by conducting a little marketing research, and if you discovered that students flock to the economics booth because they believe it provides the most assured means of making a good living, you could begin to market your English major by trumpeting the high premium multinational corporations were now placing on graduates with superb writing and analytical skills, and flog a Near Eastern Language degree by emphasizing that modern security and intelligence needs were now creating a huge demand for specialists in Arabic languages or Farsi. Or you might respond by trying to convene a meeting of your fellow academic entrepreneurs to persuade them that the good of the whole depends on a more equitable distribution of customers among the various booths and that all of you, collectively, ought to devise means of forcing customers to pass through booths to which they might not otherwise give more than a glance as they walked by.

You may recognize this last option as an intentionally cynical description of the liberal education model you find in institutions like this one. What makes it cynical is that it posits the aim of education as primarily a matter of keeping the customers flowing through the various educational shops: The aim of the philosophy major is to make sure there are philosophy majors, and a liberal education serves this aim by making sure that enough students flow through philosophy classes to allow for the possibility of persuading a few of them to make philosophy a destination rather than a way station. This would explain why liberal education might be good for philosophy, but it wouldn't make it particularly clear why philosophy may be good for us.

You have no doubt noticed my ample use of somewhat crude market-related metaphors in these remarks so far, and this is far from accidental. It is also no coincidence that the novel I've mentioned above, James's *The American,* which takes as its hero a self-made millionaire, was first published in 1877 during the era we commonly refer to as the Gilded Age—an era that itself got its label from the title of another novel, this one cowritten by Charles Dudley Warner and Mark Twain and published in 1873. *The Gilded Age* (the novel) is a broad—sometimes hilarious, sometimes painful—satire on the speculative excesses that swept the nation in the wake of the Civil War. The laying down of thousands and thousands of miles of railroad tracks (these were the years in which the transcontinental railroad was completed) touched off real estate speculation that led to an overvaluing of property, creating immense wealth for some and immediate poverty for others. The millionaire and multimillionaire, whose wealth derived from the railroads, oil, commodities trading, and the like, took up residence in the national imagination and became a prominent figure in directing national and world affairs. Likewise the modern corporation, partially as a result of the U.S. Supreme Court's interpretation of the Fourteenth Amendment to the U.S. Constitution, began rapidly transforming the economic life of the nation, leading one scholar to refer to this period as marking the "incorporation of America."[1] During these years, the U.S. Congress was known more for its scandalous behavior, cowardice, and cupidity than for its statesmanship. Accordingly towards the end of Twain and Warner's novel, a character, appropriately named Mr. Noble, who has just exposed a member of the U.S. Senate for bribery only to find that the other Senators are unlikely to pursue any punishment, cries out in indignation, "You know as well as I do that the whole nation holds as much as three-fifths of the United States Senate in entire contempt."[2] In short, according to Twain and Warner, the Gilded Age was a period when the accumulation of immense wealth by private individuals, with the collusion and sanction of those whose responsibility was to guard the public good, became the defining aim of the nation.

So let's review the score sheet: private wealth growing in both size and influence, overvalued real estate, court rulings in favor of corporate rights, cronyism in the federal government. That sounds like 1870, but it also may sound a bit like 2007. Indeed, according to some, it sounds exactly like 2007, and these critics have dubbed the period in which we've been living since the mid-1990s as the New Gilded Age. For example, ten years ago this fall, *The Baffler* magazine sponsored a national lecture and discussion series called "Business and the American Mind," which included a session entitled "The New Gilded Age." The program's announcement stated the following:

> The defining fact of American culture in the 1990s is its reorganization around the needs of the corporation. While Americans have always rallied around the titans of industry during prosperous times, never before has business managed to colonize popular imagination to such a remarkable degree.

> From the showplaces of advertising to the pronouncements of pundits, from the exalted realm of orthodox academic economics to the common wisdom of the street; the market seems to have supplanted politics, the office has become society, and the brand has been made an equivalent to human identity. As income disparities grow and the vicissitudes of the Dow eclipse the weather as smalltalk [sic] of choice, the only social justice anyone feels confident about is supposed to come through the agency of personal computers—office machines. Not only is the business of America business, the culture of America is business too.[3]

Echoing *The Baffler,* Paul Krugman, an economist and columnist for the *New York Times,* remarked on the increase in income inequality that characterizes both Gilded Ages, noting, "Well, in at least one respect, everything old is new again. Income inequality—which began rising at the same time that modern conservatism began gaining political power—is now fully back to Gilded Age levels." But I should pause here to note that Krugman's mention of "modern conservatism" makes explicit something that has been implicit in my comments and examples so far, namely the inescapably "political" dimension of any discussion about the role of wealth in shaping the affairs of the nation. Krugman observes that the late Milton Friedman, one of this university's many Nobel laureates, and Grover Norquist, architect of the Bush administration's tax cutting policies, "have portrayed the Gilded Age as a golden age, dismissing talk of the era's injustice and cruelty as a left-wing myth."[4] There may be no way of talking about these matters without someone's political ox getting gored. But that's precisely the reason we need to talk about them.

In the article from which I have been quoting, Krugman also mentions one Gilded Age figure for the purpose of comparison with today's economic moguls. That figure is John D. Rockefeller, who was an oil magnate, the richest man in the world in 1890, and, more to the point, also the University of Chicago's founder, whose memory is honored by the name of this chapel in which we are gathered today—a chapel that stands as a testament to the belief that learning, faith, and money need not be at odds with one another. I won't have the opportunity in the time allotted to me today to remark on the relationship of learning to faith, a topic very much on the mind of many at the present moment and very much worthy of some lengthy consideration. Instead I'll have to content myself with Rockefeller's hope that great wealth could serve great learning. In this hope, Rockefeller was hardly unique in his time. Other very rich men, including Leland Stanford, who founded Stanford University in 1891 with wealth amassed largely through his founding of the Central Pacific Railroad Company, and Andrew Carnegie, who founded Carnegie Mellon University in 1900 with a fortune built on Pittsburgh Steel, believed that wealth might find its true realization in great institutions of learning. Taking these men together, one could say that their lives illustrate that the ends or aims of the private accumulation of wealth was to create institutions to serve the larger good. To be sure, these men had to devote considerable time at the front end of their lives to the business of accumulation, which was often a nasty affair, requiring on occasion the bankrupting or stifling of one's competitors, the sweating of one's workers, or the expropriating of the property of those less wealthy or profitable than oneself. It was not for nothing that Rockefeller, Stanford, and these others were known as robber barons. But if at the end of the day, one could point to something like a campus on the South Side of Chicago, tricked out in impressive Gothic architecture, that had, in the span of only a decade, come to be known as one of the most prestigious institutions of higher education in the world, well, then, you just might be able to call your accounts square—and maybe, just maybe, when you consider that Rockefeller's philanthropic efforts went well beyond the University of Chicago and included, among other things, helping to found Spelman College for African American women—maybe you could even come out a little ahead.

So, if the aim of the private accumulation of great wealth is to create institutions, like this one—that is, institutions that serve the larger good—then it would follow that the end or aim of the education offered in an institution like this one is to serve the larger good. So, there you have it: The aim of education is to serve the larger good. Period. End of story. I could probably drop in the University's motto at this juncture, "Let knowledge grow from more to more; and so be human life enriched," and take a bow, and we could all be on our way, with me not even halfway through the time I've been allotted. This is the kind of efficiency that might have made old Rockefeller himself proud.

In truth, I'd love to stop here, but something won't let me apply the brakes. And that something happens to be this notion of "the greater good." Just what is it, and how is it to be reckoned? Is it a simple numerical calculation? If not, who gets to determine it? These questions are particularly pertinent given that one assumption these men made in constructing their empires was that some level of inequality was compatible with, and even necessary to, the achievement of the higher ends represented by education and culture. Carnegie, in his well-known essay, "Wealth," which was retitled and more popularly circulated as "The Gospel of Wealth," wrote:

> The contrast between the palace of the millionaire and the cottage of the laborer with us to-day measures the change which has come with civilization.
>
> This change, however, is not to be deplored, but welcomed as highly beneficial. It is well, nay, essential for the progress of the race, that the houses of some should be homes for all that is highest and best in literature and the arts, and for all the refinements of civilization, rather than that none should be so.[5]

With Carnegie's words in mind, the question I'd have to put to these robber barons is that if by their own admission the private accumulation of wealth requires great disparities that presume a "contrast between the palace of the millionaire and the cottage of the laborer," then how does this count as the greater good? Or to ask the question somewhat differently, might there be a good greater than this greater good?

Carnegie's answer is no—at least not in the world in which he operates. For him, the only imaginable alternative to a world in which some have a lot and others only a little is a world in which everyone is stuck with only a little. As he writes:

> But even if we admit . . . that it is a nobler ideal that man should labor, not for himself alone, but in and for a brother-

> hood of his fellows, and share with them all in common, realizing Swedenborg's idea of Heaven, where, as he says, the angels derive their happiness, not from laboring for self, but for each other,—even admit all this, and a sufficient answer is, This is not evolution, but revolution. It necessitates the changing of human nature itself a work of aeons, even if it were good to change it, which we cannot know. It is not practicable in our day or in our age. Even if desirable theoretically, it belongs to another and long-succeeding sociological stratum. Our duty is with what is practicable now; with the next step possible in our day and generation. It is criminal to waste our energies in endeavoring to uproot, when all we can profitably or possibly accomplish is to bend the universal tree of humanity a little in the direction most favorable to the production of good fruit under existing circumstances. We might as well urge the destruction of the highest existing type of man because he failed to reach our ideal as favor the destruction of Individualism, Private Property, the Law of Accumulation of Wealth, and the Law of Competition; for these are the highest results of human experience, the soil in which society so far has produced the best fruit. Unequally or unjustly, perhaps, as these laws sometimes operate, and imperfect as they appear to the Idealist, they are, nevertheless, like the highest type of man, the best and most valuable of all that humanity has yet accomplished.[6]

This is quite a statement and much can be said about it, but for now I'll paraphrase it as follows in regard to the goals of this evening's lecture: According to Carnegie, who I'll take as speaking for his fellow philanthropist/millionaires, the aim of private higher education is to demonstrate that the conditions conducing to the private accumulation of wealth produce achievements and goods that are unmatched by any other imaginable system. And since this will be an important point that we'll have to test, I'll repeat it: the aim of private higher education is to demonstrate that the conditions conducing to the private accumulation of wealth produce achievements and goods that are unmatched by any other imaginable system. And for good measure I'll rephrase it more crudely: "Sure," Carnegie says, "we may have more poverty than some of you think is justifiable but as a consequence we also have some of the best universities in the world." At this moment perhaps both you and I are wishing that I'd found the brake when I hit upon "the greater good" answer, which sounded so much more uplifting. If it seemed cynical for me to suggest earlier that the aim of a liberal arts education is to make sure that there are enough customers for the various humanities disciplines that might otherwise not draw very well on their own, now I'm saying that the aim of having a topflight philosophy department or history department or whatever is to demonstrate the superiority of our system of capital accumulation, despite its flaws, over any other system. This would not be because these departments as such are interested directly in providing such a justification, but rather because we know that societies are measured by their capacity to produce topflight intellects. Thus, if we want our society to be deemed a worthy one, we have to produce a requisite number of topflight intellects. On this view, it doesn't much matter what these intellects actually do, only that they be acknowledged as topflight. Once again though, if part of my purpose here is to inspire you, I have to confess that so far I don't think I've done a very good job. Nonetheless I'm asking for your patience because, as so often happens in melodramatic narratives in which good and evil do battle, the hero (who is, in this context, inspiration) is sure to show up just in the nick of time. In the meantime, though, we also have to figure out whether or not what I've said about the aim of education is: (A) True; (B) Ideology; (C) A description of the Chicago economics department; (D) All of the above; or (E) None of the above. (And I bet no one told you there was going to be a quiz tonight.)

Before moving on to answer this question, though, I think it's important to add a little more by way of context. The monumental philanthropic efforts that led not only to the founding of the great universities I have mentioned, but also to the development of modern philanthropy itself were not produced ab ovo from the minds of these titans themselves. Rather, these philanthropic ventures were at least in part responses to the fact that the unprecedented growth of the new economy of the Gilded Age had also produced significant immiserization among members of the working population, many of whom did indeed believe that there might be a viable alternative to the capitalist order that was in the process of securing its dominance. Carnegie, in composing "Wealth," was writing explicitly against the doctrines of socialism and communism and the fear that these ideas might find adherents not only among the working classes but also among the educated classes. Secondly, as attested to by the number of authors during the first Gilded Age who noted the mesmerizing appeal of accumulation for the sake of accumulation, these efforts were occurring at a moment when, in the eyes of many observers, the American genius of making lots of money had not demonstrated its capacity to do much beyond accumulate heretofore unimaginable amounts of capital.

For example, in describing Christopher Newman, the hero of *The American,* Henry James writes:

> It must be admitted, rather nakedly, that Christopher Newman's sole aim in life had been to make money; what he had been placed in the world for was, to his own perception, simply to wrest a fortune, the bigger the better, from defiant opportunity. This idea completely filled his horizon and satisfied his imagination. Upon the uses of money upon what one might do with a life into which one had succeeded in injecting the golden stream, he had to up to his thirtyfifth year very scantily reflected. Life had been for him an open game, and he had played for high stakes. He had won at last and carried off his winnings; and now what to do with them?[7]

In a similar vein, W. E. B. DuBois, writing in 1903, warned southern Americans that:

> Atlanta must not lead the South to dream of material prosperity as the touchstone of all success; already the fatal might of this idea is beginning to spread; it is replacing the finer type of Southerner with vulgar money-getters; it is burying the sweeter beauties of Southern life beneath pretence and ostentation. For every social ill the panacea of Wealth has been urged,—wealth to overthrow the remains of the slave feudalism; wealth to raise

> the "cracker" Third Estate; wealth to employ the black serfs, and the prospect of wealth to keep them working; wealth as the end and aim of politics, and as the legal tender for law and order; and, finally, instead of Truth, Beauty, and Goodness, wealth as the ideal of the public school.[8]

And here is Henry James again, in his 1903 book, *The American Scene,* which he wrote after returning to the United States following an absence of some twenty years, describing the New York City skyscrapers:

> Crowned not only with no history, but with no credible possibility of time for history, and consecrated by no uses save the commercial at any cost, they are simply the most piercing notes in that concert of the expensively provisional into which your supreme sense of New York resolves itself. They never begin to speak to you, in the manner of the builded majesties of the world as we have heretofore known such—towers or temples or fortresses or palaces—with the authority of things of permanence or even of things of long duration. One story is good only till another is told, and sky-scrapers are the last word of economic ingenuity only till another word be written.[9]

I could go on, but I hope you see the point. Taken together, these passages reveal that in the eyes of some of the most astute cultural observers at the time, the genius of the American economic order had yet to demonstrate itself capable of producing a culture capable of rivaling those of the feudal, aristocratic, and paternalistic societies that had preceded it.

This may be a criticism that is a little bit difficult to credit at this moment early in the twenty-first century when many are inclined to speak of U.S. cultural dominance, and scholars and intellectuals from around the world flock to our shores. Nonetheless, for many expatriate and virtually expatriate writers and artists from the late nineteenth through the early twentieth centuries, the United States did not offer conditions necessary to any aims higher than those of Wall Street or Main Street. So the ability of American wealth to justify itself by adducing evidence that it was interested in aims other than its own aggrandizement has been a very recent phenomenon, and institutions like the University of Chicago have played no small role in establishing the basis for this justification.

But this might be a good time to go back to my quiz, which asked whether the second claim I've made about the aim of education is (A) True; (B) Ideology; (C) A description of the Chicago economics department; (D) All of the above; or (E) None of the above. Well, among the first things you'll learn here is that truth and ideology are at once different things and the same thing. We usually think of truth as referring to the way things in the world really are and ideology as referring to the way some interested party claims things in the world ought to be, despite evidence to the contrary. Truth, we like to say, is a matter of fact, and ideology is a matter of value. What makes the distinction difficult to sustain, though, is that ideology also denotes the way that ideas work in and on the world, shaping the reality around us. Truths change, and they do so often as a result of the efforts of people armed with ideas and beliefs to change reality. For example, a shared conviction of many Gilded Age novelists was that the practice of novel writing had to change because the reality that these novelists were charged with representing was changing around them, and if novels derived their authority from the accuracy of their representations of how humans behaved in the world, then novelists were going to have to persuade their readers that their stories accurately represented the way economic forces were changing human behavior. A novel that seemed perfectly adequate to the world of 1855 might feel antiquated in the world of 1875.

Of course, the world around us is not infinitely accommodating of the ideas we have about it, or of our desires for it to be one way rather than another, or of the representations we make of it. Reality pushes back, and it is at this point of push back that truth and ideology often part company—the place where the world will not conform to our desire.

But I've delayed too long in deciding the possible correctness of options (A) and (B); and, as you've probably guessed, I'm going to say that both (A) and (B) are at least a little correct. Certainly in the views of their founders, these major universities were created in part to vindicate the wealth that had produced them, so my assertion that the aim of education is to justify the conditions that conduce to the private accumulation of wealth does have some claim on historical truth. What makes this statement ideological though (ideological, that is, in the sense of being a statement that attempts to represent the University in a certain way for my own ends) is that it is somewhat reductive. After all, every one of these universities has been home to scholars representing a variety of viewpoints, many of which are and have been critical of the prevailing order and of the conditions that produced it. What makes a great university great is that once you put it together by saying to the philosophers, "I don't care what you do as long as you are regarded by those who know philosophy as doing it better than anyone else in the world," you inevitably open up the possibility that your philosophers will say things that you don't like—things that bring into question the truths and justifications you think they ought to be affirming. So if it were correct to say that the aim of higher education is to justify the material conditions of its production, it would also be correct to say that the aim of higher education is to create conditions that allow for the criticism of the conditions of private accumulation, and of everything else under the sun. So much for options (A) and (B).

What about option (C): the possibility that my assertion is merely a description of the Chicago economics department? Here I'm on dangerous turf indeed. Not only will a plurality of the students in this audience become economics majors (I'm also proud to say that not an insubstantial number of you will become English majors), but, as you all know, as measured by Nobel Prizes and other awards conferred, ours is the best economics department in the world and is one of the best departments at this university. There's another mundane reason I ought to tread carefully here: the most direct indoor route from my office in the English department to the nearest coffee shop takes me first through the economics department and then through the philosophy department. (It may be that my coffee habit also explains why the philosophy department has loomed so large in my examples here.) So, if I don't want to get waylaid by disgruntled colleagues when I shamble down the hallway in pursuit of a cup of decaf, I'd better watch what I say.

It is certainly true that much of the current and most respected work that has come out of our economics department has provided arguments or evidence supporting policies that favor private enterprise over government intervention in many areas of human endeavor. The debate about privatizing Social Security, for example, is taking place not only in the halls of Congress but also in the scholarly papers written by Chicago scholars. And if Carnegie argued in the early twentieth century that inequality was necessary for human progress, our Nobel Prize-winning economics professor Gary S. Becker has recently argued in a paper co-authored with Kevin M. Murphy that "an increase in earnings inequality due primarily to higher rates of return on education and other skills [should] be considered a favorable rather than an unfavorable development" because "[h]igher rates of return on capital are a sign of greater productivity in the economy, and that inference is fully applicable to human capital as well as to physical capital. The initial impact of higher returns to human capital is wider inequality in earnings (the same as the initial effect of higher returns on physical capital), but that impact becomes more muted and may be reversed over time as young men and women invest more in their human capital."[10]

Of course one professor does not a department make, nor one quotation an argument. Professor Becker's article, for example, does not say that all inequality is good or that we shouldn't be concerned about the nature, duration, or the degree of inequality. Neither do his views represent those of every professor in the economics department, some of whom have addressed inequality in a variety of ways. But the crucial point to be made here is that Professor Becker is not making this argument simply because he would like it to be true. He is making it because he believes that the data, evidence, and methodology employed demonstrate it to be true regardless of what he or anyone else may want to believe. So then, to return to my quiz, option (C), which posits that the vindication of private accumulation stands as a description of the economics department, is not quite right if this statement means to suggest that some of the professors in that department are willing to insist on this conclusion come hell or high water. Rather, the conclusions reached by these scholars are a function of the methodological operations they employ. As the economics department Web site states quite eloquently regarding its various areas of emphases, "The unifying thread in all this is not political or ideological but methodological, the methodological conviction that economics is an incomparably powerful tool for understanding society."[11] It is true that some skeptical observer might want to say that if your methodology repeatedly produces conclusions that conform to the idea of the world you find most congenial, then there might be reason to question your ability to distinguish between method and ideology—what, after all, is meant by that wonderful phrase "methodological conviction?" This objection, however, raises more questions than I can pursue at present.

But finally to finish up my quiz, it seems that answers (A), (B), and (C) are each partly right and partly wrong, which would then make answers (D) "All of the above" and (E) "None of the above" also partly right and partly wrong. So it's all a muddle: I haven't given you fully persuasive reasons to discount my cynical formulation of the aim of higher education, nor have I given you fully persuasive reasons to buy it. But don't despair—I promised to get us back on a more inspiring track, and I mean to make good on this promise before I finish. And to do so, first I'll take you back a half step to the marvelous audacity of the statement that I quoted from the Web site of the economics department: ". . . the methodological conviction that economics is an incomparably powerful tool for understanding society." In addition to "conviction," the words that stand out for me are "incomparably powerful." The members of the department could have described economics as a "very useful" tool, a "pretty damn good tool," or "one of many necessary tools" for understanding society, but they decided instead to swing for the fences and go with "incomparably powerful tool." It would follow, then, that they hold the tools employed by other disciplines to explain human behavior to be comparably less powerful. I, frankly, think they have every right to make this claim, not because I'm sure I agree with it but because I think it is useful as a guide to what the aim of education ought to be at the present moment.

Simply put, this aim is to get you to entertain the possibility that there might be tools—some new, some perhaps out of fashion—for understanding society that are possibly better than the ones we are now employing. Of course, in order for you to determine what makes one tool better or worse than another, you must first understand the nature of the tools currently in use. This necessity is what makes a liberal education the valuable thing it is. It requires that you gain more than a passing acquaintance with the methods that define inquiry in different fields so that you can get a sense of both their scope and their limitations. More precisely this is also what makes the idea of the Core Curriculum at Chicago so valuable. The Core is premised in part on the conviction that there are key critical skills necessary not only to prepare you to master a discipline once you've decided which one you'd like to take up but also to give you the capacity to view your chosen discipline from a point a little bit outside of its claims and justifications. This "outsider perspective" is important because to believe in the incomparable power of a disciplinary methodology is to take ideas quite seriously. (And if there's anything that defines the University of Chicago, it is taking ideas seriously.) To take one's ideas seriously is to believe that they will produce good results when applied to the world. Ideas have consequences, and before you commit to these consequences you might indeed want to hear from the wielders of other methodological tools what they think about the understanding of society you claim to have confirmed.

You may or may not know that in the 1940s the Carnegie Corporation, using the work of sociologists trained at the University of Chicago, commissioned a massive study of U.S. race relations, under the direction of Swedish sociologist Gunnar Myrdal. Titled *An American Dilemma,* this study shaped American racial policy for the next several decades. You may or may not know that in the 1970s after the Chilean coup by Augusto Pinochet a "group of economists known as 'the Chicago boys' because of their attachment to the neoliberal theories of Milton Friedman, then teaching [here] at the University of Chicago, was summoned to help reconstruct the Chilean economy."[12] You may or may not know that one of Paul Bremer's goals in Iraq as stated in the "Coalition Provisional Authority Order Number 39: Foreign Investment" was to assist in the "transition from a non-transparent centrally planned economy to a market economy characterized by sustainable economic growth through the establishment of a dynamic private sector, and the need to enact institutional and legal reforms to give it effect."[13] You may not, until now, have known about these things, but, after you have learned about them, how you assess the consequences that ensued from those attempts to put ideas into action will depend on your certainty that these were indeed the best ideas available.

I'm not prepared to declare the novels I study and teach "incomparably powerful tools for understanding society." I think they happen to be pretty good ones, though. For example, one can take another Gilded Age novel, Mark Twain's *A Connecticut Yankee in King Arthur's Court,* which imaginatively transports its protagonist, Hank Morgan, who is a foreman in a nineteenth-century weapons factory, into the medieval world of King Arthur's Court, with the dream of reconstructing that society on the basis of democratic government, technological innovation, and free-market principles. The power and genius of the novel derive from Twain's ability to have the satire cut both ways, exposing both the limits and cruelties of the society Morgan wishes to reform as well as the hubris and blindness of the society that thinks itself better than all others. I won't say much more for fear of spoiling it for those who've not yet read it, but I do have to say that things, of course, do not go well for Hank who finds himself trapped in a prison of his own making. Twain is far from having the last word about how to think about restructuring a society other than one's own, but he does have insights worth considering for anyone who finds herself or himself faced with the decision of whether or not to support such an effort.

The challenges awaiting you at the University of Chicago are the challenges posed by powerful ideas, some of which were produced with the aim of bringing the whole of human action into their ambit. Our shared responsibility is to gain the capacity to understand these ideas, to critique them, and, when necessary, to wield them with wisdom and self-reflection. And beyond this, it also falls to us to contemplate the possibility of, and to assist in the creation of, new ideas so that we, like James's Christopher Newman, but without the burden of having to pile up riches beforehand, can give way to the "vague sense that more answers were possible than [our philosophies] had hitherto dreamt of." There, I hope you're feeling a little better now.

I want to thank you again for your attention and patience. Please accept my best wishes for your future here at the University of Chicago. ❍

KENNETH W. WARREN, the Fairfax M. Cone Distinguished Service Professor in the Department of English Language & Literature, the Committees on African & African American Studies and History of Culture, and the College; and Deputy Provost for Research and Minority Issues, delivered this address on September 20, 2007.

ENDNOTES

1. Alan Trachtenberg, *The Incorporation of America: Culture and Society in the Gilded Age* (New York: Hill and Wang, 2007).

2. Mark Twain and Charles Dudley Warner, *The Gilded Age: A Tale of Today* (New York: Signet, 1969), p. 411.

3. Business and the American Mind: A national lecture and discussion series organized by *The Baffler* magazine, October–November 1997. *http://www.press.uchicago.edu/News/971008pr.html*

4. Paul Krugman, "Gilded Once More," *New York Times* (April 27, 2007). *http://select.nytimes.com/2007/04/27/opinion/27krugman.html*

5. Andrew Carnegie, "Wealth," *North American Review* CCCXCL.391 (June 1889), p. 653.

6. *Ibid.* p. 656.

7. Henry James, *The American,* ed. James W. Tuttleton (New York: W. W. Norton, 1978), p. 32.

8. W. E. B. DuBois, *The Souls of Black Folk,* in *Writings* (New York: Library of America), p. 417.

9. James, *The American Scene* (Bloomington, IN: Indiana University Press, 1968), p. 77.

10. Gary S. Becker and Kevin M. Murphy, "The Upside of Income Inequality," *The American: A Magazine of Ideas* (May/June 2007). *http://www.american.com/archive/2007/may-june-magazine-contents/the-upside-of-income-inequality?searchterm=becker*

11. The University of Chicago Department of Economics, "About the Department." *http://economics.uchicago.edu/about.shtml*

12. David Harvey, *A Brief History of Neoliberalism* (New York: Oxford University Press, 2005), p. 6.

13. See Harvey, p. 6, and Coalition Provisional Authority Order Number 39: Foreign Investment, CPA/ORD/19 September 2003/39. *http://www.export.gov/iraq/pdf/cpa_order_80.pdf*

 Published in 2009
Printed in the United States of America

Produced for the Dean of the College

For additional copies, contact the Dean of the College
1116 East 59th Street, Chicago, Illinois 60637